FINDING STABILITY AND PURPOSE IN JESUS

WHO AM I AND WHAT AM I DOING WITH MY LIFE?

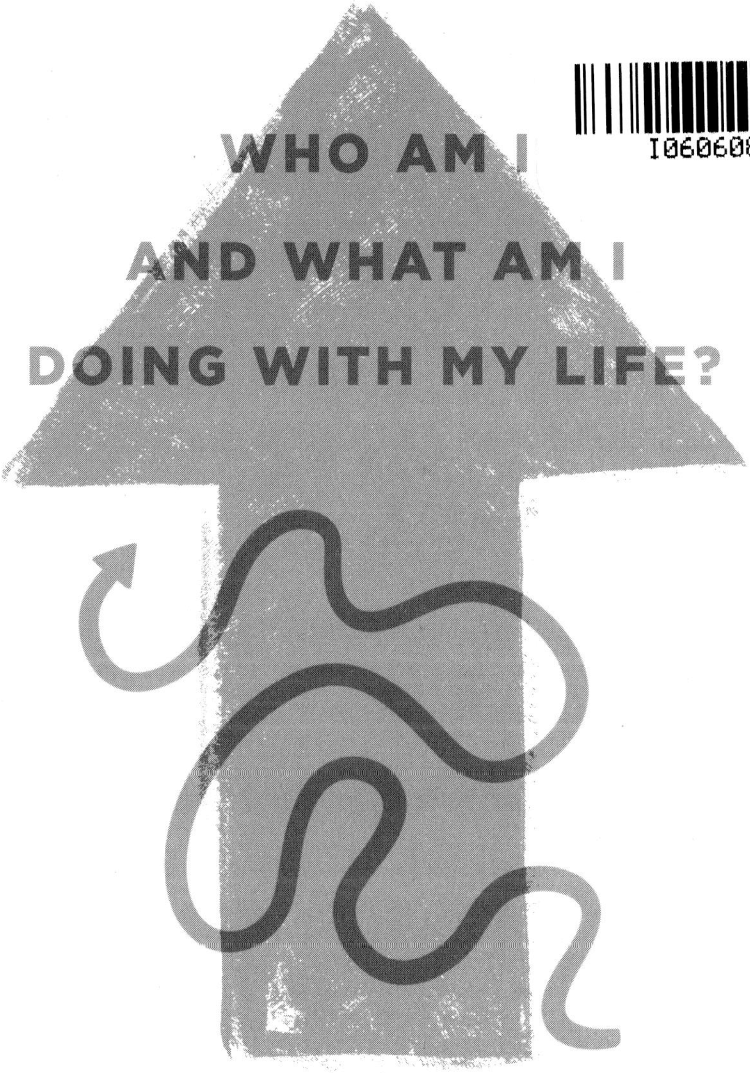

JUSTIN N. POYTHRESS

thegoodbook COMPANY

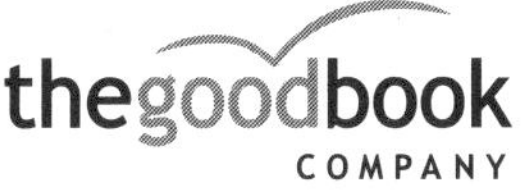

Who Am I and What Am I Doing with My Life?
Finding Stability and Purpose in Jesus

Published by:
The Good Book Company

thegoodbook.com | thegoodbook.co.uk
thegoodbook.com.au | thegoodbook.co.nz

Cover design by Faceout Studio | Design and art direction by André Parker

ISBN: 9781802544183 | JOB-008575 | Printed in India

Dedicated to Liz,
who helps me become who I am in Jesus.

Contents

CHAPTER 1

Who Are You?

Luke is twenty-five. He grew up in Chicago but moved to New York City a couple years ago because… why not? He was still young, so it was the time to do it. He got a job as a bartender while he looked for work using his degree in digital design. About a year ago, he started feeling adrift. What *did* he want to do? What if art never pays the bills? Some friends have gotten married and moved away. Some friends have just given up and moved back home. Luke knows he's got a lot to offer—he's good with people. He's good at art and design. He's funny. He can work hard. But none of this has seemed to translate into anything. He's just getting older. Maybe he should just move back home too.

Andrea is eighteen. Her dad is a navy officer, a few years from retirement. She's spent her whole childhood moving, never staying anywhere longer than two or three years. She's loved the diversity of people she's been around—different ethnicities, religions, and cultures. She has learned to fit in with any group. She can small talk about hair and makeup, and she can geek out about Greek mythology. But being a master chameleon means she isn't really sure who she is. Her family has always attended church regularly, and this part of her identity tends to shut her out of the most popular circles. Her dad's most recent assignment was in Florida, so Andrea enrolled in the University of Central Florida—the largest, most diverse university she could find. She'll be starting over yet again. Which side of herself should she lead with? Which groups should she attach to, and how deeply? There is almost no one that she *couldn't* be.

Trent just turned thirty-three. He's been married for a couple of years, and he couldn't have imagined a better partner. He and his wife are aligned politically and religiously. They're both intelligent, successful, and upwardly mobile in their careers, with no children. Trent's been working like a dog for the past three years to make partner at his law firm. But as the finish line is coming into view, panic is setting in. Trent has begun seeing the current partners in a new light. Is this the life he really wants? Breaking away from the firm and starting over at this stage seems terrifying, but so does the prospect of cementing himself in this job and closing off all his other options. Does he want kids? What if he and his wife plant their roots but forever miss this window of risking something new? Trent and his wife were both brought up in Christian homes, but it's all started to feel a bit stale. He wonders whether church is really doing much for them or if they're just going out of habit.

All three of these individuals are slightly altered versions of real people. The situations and the pressure points are different, but the angst is the same: *Is this who I should be? Is this where I should be? Or what I should be doing? Did I miss something?*

We live in a world of endless possibilities. There's never been more freedom to create your own identity—you can go where you want, do what you want, marry who you want. You can basically create a life and even your personhood from scratch, almost like an avatar. You can reinvent yourself a hundred times if you want to, which means identity pressure has never felt more intense. Sometimes the open-endedness of life can feel like opportunity, but other times it feels like self-doubt and missing out. The range of possibilities is paralyzing.

We're most likely to feel the panic of this realization when we arrive at a pivotal moment—considering a career change, or whether to propose or to move away from home. Sometimes we feel it at a particular age; sociologist Brian Rosner calls this "cuspiety." It's the crisis that comes in reaching a cusp age (19, 29, 59) and feeling unsure about what life is, what comes next, and who you are.[1]

But why wait for a year ending in nine? That sounds like my agenda tomorrow. Identity crises aren't just for the girl in her late twenties living at home and waiting tables, or the corporate drone who sold his soul for a health insurance plan and suburban grass thicker than his hair. Sometimes all it takes is someone else's photo, relationship status update, Christmas card, or casual remark about a milestone we haven't achieved, to plunge us into the same old questions: *who am I really, and what on earth am I doing with my life?*

So how do you find peace and certainty while you feel like you're running around a labyrinth full of dead ends? How do you make the right choices and become the person you want to be? That's what this book is all about.

I don't know what your "what ifs" are. Maybe you're young and feeling overwhelmed by all the options ahead of you. Maybe you're older and filled with regret as you look back. Maybe your sense of instability is career-related or has to do with marriage, or maybe it just stems from spending time online looking at how perfect everybody else's lives seem to be.

Whatever your particular version of this looks like, though, I have something that I think will help.

Your identity will always be in flux. Circumstances and relationships change. You change. But in the midst of all that, God has a stable identity for you that makes sense of everything else. It's an identity centered on Christ. When you begin to see that as your fixed point, other things come into focus. You can relax and trust because you see where God is taking you. When you understand the identity project God is working on in you, it will give you a sense of confidence and peace about who you are and who you are becoming. You really can feel secure even while the world around you is churning, fraught with weighty decisions and potential wrong turns. The Bible says that Christians will spend a lifetime discovering the riches of the mystery that is their identity: "Christ in you, the hope of glory" (Colossians 1:27). In Jesus, you have a glorious identity that keeps getting better.

We're going to talk about Jesus some more later in this chapter. But first, in order to get a better sense of yourself and the direction you should be going, we need to understand a little more what identity is.

What Is Identity? (It's Complicated)

Your identity is your sense of self. It involves looking inside yourself to evaluate who you are and what you're like. You're a Brazilian, a musician, an engineer, a father.

But identity isn't just about how you would describe yourself right now. It also has a backward-looking and a forward-looking component. That's why a one-year-old boy who lives in the present will have rather little to say about his identity—he's not looking backward into his past or forward to his future. But one day, when he's a little older, he'll look back and say, "I've always been talkative"—or he'll look forward and say, "I want to be a firefighter when I grow up."

Identity discussions, then, are a push-pull between understanding who you are as a product of the past and who you wish to be in the future. Still, the question of the future always sits in the driver's seat. Even if you're doing some kind of deep dive down the rabbit hole of your subconscious, you're doing it for the sake of your future. *How will what I discover help me live better tomorrow?*

Another way to say this is that you are both *being* and *becoming*. You are stable and growing. You will get edgy if you feel like someone is trying to pin you down to only one of those aspects. Imagine that when you were seven, you were proud to show your Uncle Steve that you learned to juggle. That was great back then—but you're not too pleased that he continues to introduce you as "my niece, the juggler." Your identity isn't just about that one element of your past! It's the same with your future. Let's say that every time you visit your grandma, she hints that she's available for daycare as soon as you find that someone special. *Sure, maybe one day I'll have kids, Grandma, but that's not what my life is about right now!*

This desire for being and becoming (an identity that's both stable and growing) is why models and professional athletes often have such a hard time later in life. On the one hand, when you're fifty, you don't want everyone to forget that you were a world-class tennis player—to feel like the identity that you devoted twelve hours a day, twenty-five years of your life to was a waste and you're already a footnote. But a perpetual recognition of your past can also keep you trapped—as if no one is interested in or even *wants* you to become something other than "the tennis player."

We all feel like this to some degree, world-class tennis player or not. We're caught between two desires. You long to feel that parts of you are stable and good and valuable—these are the things that make you who you are. And yet you want to be growing and maturing, open to change and development. This dual desire intersects every aspect of your identity. We want a stable sense of self but without feeling boxed in by it. We want our lives to look like the title of Michelle Obama's autobiography—one long upward journey of *Becoming*. We want to be rooted but growing. How can you be both?

Given these competing desires and realities, here's a definition of identity:

Identity is your sense of self
that connects who you are as a product of your past
with who you wish to be in the future.

But before we figure out how to find stability between these forward-looking and backward-looking aspects, you need to understand something more about yourself. Or should I say, your *selves*.

Identities of Origin, Role, and Affinity

Imagine several people are gathered in a room. There's a nine-year-old boy who loves to draw and dance to Kanye West and who uses the words "et cetera" a lot. There's also an intelligent, middle-aged man with OCD who touches everything with a yellow rag and also has a track record of abuse. There's a cussing but kind-hearted teenage girl who takes insulin shots for her diabetes. And there's a tenured professor who specializes in 1950s-80s Japanese cinema. Here's the twist: they are all the same person.

This is M. Night Shyamalan's thriller *Split*, in which the antagonist suffers from dissociative identity disorder (formerly multiple personality disorder). He has twenty-three distinct personalities living within him, each one complete with its own mannerisms, accents, and even health conditions. The movie builds towards the emergence of a twenty-fourth personality—a beast with superhuman strength. And although you're unlikely to identify as a mythical beast, Shyamalan plays with a question that haunts all of us—who are you, really? Maybe it feels like you could be any one of at least eight different personalities. Which one is the real you? And who else *could* you be if you set your mind to it?

This is why your identity feels complex and confusing. You're never just one thing. A better way to think about your self is that you have dozens, even hundreds of "identities" or "selves" inside of you. Each of them is valid, but each one of them only tells part of the story.

I don't want this to sound weird. I'm only one person. There's only one name on my ID card—Justin N. Poythress. But I can also talk about my identity as a husband, a pastor, a Dallas Cowboys fan, and the kind of person who loves coffee and craft root beer. I have one (somewhat) unified identity composed of multiple sub-identities. Sociologists have collected ten traditional identity markers: race, ethnicity and nationality; gender and sexuality; physical and mental capacity; religion; cultural background; family of origin; close relationships; occupations; possessions; and age.[2]

I believe we can think about identity in three basic layers of "sub-identities." To be clear, I'm not a sociologist. I don't think I'm creating something new. Human nature doesn't change. I've simply attempted to come up with some categorical terms to package the various elements of identity that we all reference when we talk about it in the 21st century. These three layers of identity are identities of origin, identities of role, and identities of affinity.

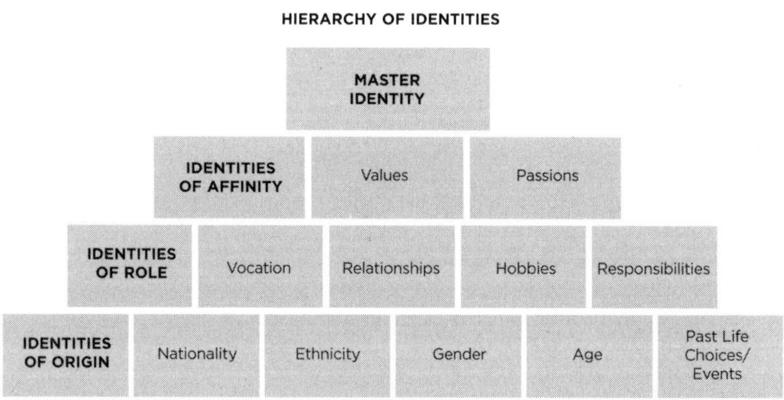

Identities of Origin

We get all our big identities of origin at birth. They include things like ethnicity, gender, nationality, time and place of birth, parents, and lineage. As life goes on, your identity of origin continues to collect more historical, objective identity-shaping events—both ones you have chosen and ones that have just happened to you. Let's say you're born in Hong Kong, but you move to London at age five. If you haven't moved again by age ten, London has now become another significant identity of origin. Also, that time when you were eight and your neighbor's German Shepherd escaped and chased you four blocks up the street—that event has become an identity of origin that shapes how you view strange dogs.

Identities of Role

Identities of role have to do with responsibilities. Responsibilities are tied to relationships. You might have a role as an uncle, aunt, son, grandmother, boss, employee, volunteer, colleague, or friend. Sometimes you wear more than one hat at the same time. The importance of any given role in your identity has to do with the weight you feel *from* that responsibility. For example, one of my roles at home is doing the dishes. But I will not request the epitaph:

Justin
Unloader of the dishwasher

I'm hoping it's not that important.

Your roles span all kinds of activities including vocations, hobbies, and services. You could be a student, nanny, golfer, lawyer, or handyman. You slide in and out of roles over your lifetime or within a given day. We don't live our lives basking in the reflective zen of a weekend retreat on personality types. A role like driver-of-a-car, though it may not seem substantive, matters a good deal when you get behind that wheel. Your roles are like one of those sensory pin boards that holds the impression of your hand or nose. A role rises or falls in its prominence depending on how hard you press on it.

Identities of Affinity

If you think in terms of stable and growing, your identities of affinity are the ones that grow and change the most. This category includes anything someone is passionate about. Obviously, that changes. Passions rise, recede, or vanish altogether. You have a long runway to gather speed; then, before you know it, you're flying around the world in your passion plane. The question becomes: what other part of life or society will you visit with that passion? And where will you not just visit but take up residence, and put that passion to work?

Affinity is the outermost layer of identity—the one we most easily put on or discard. But when you decide to wear an affinity with pride, it's the first thing people will notice about you. Identities of affinity include things like playing tennis, watching *The Office*, political parties, religious affiliations, your favorite musical artist, or fitness or nutrition lifestyles. An identity of affinity has the most intrinsic ability to seize command over your whole life. As an identity of affinity grows in importance, it will start doing big things, like shaping your community and your values, and reshuffling your schedule.

You've probably spotted the difficulty. Identities can overlap into two or all three of these categories. Your love for animals starts off as an identity of affinity but becomes an identity of role if you become a veterinarian. Your time spent in Peru as a child (an identity of origin) turns into a lifelong interest in Latin American cuisine (an identity of affinity). And so on.

These identities grow and shrink in importance over time. Your sense of self today differs from how you experienced it yesterday. Or for that matter, two hours ago. There are different events, pressures, and desires weighing on you right now that push you toward one package of sub-identities versus another. And even if you zero in on one sub-identity that you decide you will emphasize throughout your whole life, like being a mother, what that identity means to you will also change over time.

Life can feel like one long game of five-card poker. You can only hold five cards in your hand at one time, but you're always drawing, discarding, rearranging, or restarting in order to work your way toward a winning hand at *that* specific moment.

One Identity to Rule Them All—A Master Identity

In the poker game of life (unlike in M. Night Shyamalan's *Split*), you do realize that you are only *one person* holding all these cards—one person making all these decisions. This is where a "master identity" comes in. A master identity gives you the stability you need to navigate your changing circumstances and your shifting and developing sub-identities. A master identity is also subject to change, but this happens more slowly and deliberately than with your other identities. An easy way to boil it down in your own mind is to force yourself to fill in this blank with one word: I am a ____________. Whatever you put there is your master identity.

A master identity is like the CEO running the company of your self. It promotes one sub-identity and fires another. It hands out bonuses and growth plans. Let's say your master identity is "artsy filmmaker." It gives a corner office to that part of you that collects Alfred Hitchcock memorabilia. Meanwhile, it stuffs your suburban, summer-sports-camp upbringing into the basement to file paperwork.

This master identity works as a sort of interpretive grid for how you see the world and interact with others. For example, let's say you have a friend who got into the keto diet and went a little bit overboard. It's now become his master identity. You'll be talking about your car leaking coolant, and he'll pipe up, "That's what I felt like till I cut out the carbs." The keto diet is now his response to everything!

You can see how important a master identity is. In fact, having a master identity is the only way we can make sense of all these selves we've got inside of us. And ideally, we need a good one. The keto diet is not going to be enough to reconcile all these competing identities. Nor is being an artsy filmmaker.

But Jesus *will* be enough.

The Answer

In Romans 8:29, God explains his identity plan for every Christian for all time: he "predestined [us] to be conformed to the image of his Son."

With Jesus, you receive a new identity—or, more accurately, you receive a resurrected identity. Who you are, at your deepest level, is now connected to Jesus. And you're becoming more like Jesus—less sinful, more godly. You're being conformed to his image.

There is a sense in which the Christian life is *all about* identity. It's about discovering and recovering who you were really designed to be.

God intentionally designed you the way that you are—with your personality, background, gifts, and talents. Yet you and I are far from being what we could be. We make bad choices; we act as the worst version of ourselves; we go off on the wrong track.

But in Christ, you are becoming more of who you are supposed to be. That's what God is up to in your life.

As you live connected to Jesus, God enters your unique origins, roles, and affinities, and builds you up through those things. He may alter the identities that you find most important, but he will always be leading you on an upward journey. You will become a more "life-sized" version of you. You will get to discover who you *really* are and what you're *really* made for. You'll still spend the rest of your life growing and becoming. You'll still wonder what your next choice should be. But no matter what, this image of Jesus that you're moving toward *never* changes.

When you understand that transformation isn't merely the process but also the purpose of what God is up to in your life, your sense of identity will feel stable even while it grows.

Questions for Discussion and Reflection

1. What situations have led you to questions about your identity? Why?
2. Think about one aspect of your identity. In what way is this connected with your past and future? How does your future vision of yourself have an impact on what's important to your identity today?
3. How would the master identity of a relationship with Jesus reshape your perspective on the other parts of your identity?

CHAPTER 2

Where Are You Going?

It was April. I would start my final year of college in the fall. I remember the stomach-churning disbelief I felt as I sat in an office with an advisor planning out what coursework I needed to graduate. I walked back to my dormitory room in a stupor. I kept rerunning the numbers, hoping we'd got the math wrong. I had thought that in my final year, I'd coast to the finish line. Now I saw that if I took a normal courseload, I'd end up just short of the requirements to graduate.

How had this happened? I didn't change majors. I hadn't taken any useless electives like "Anthropology of *Toy Story*." Somehow, my previous advisors and I simply hadn't been looking at the end goal. I'd assumed I was on the right track and just did the next thing.

I ended up taking extra courses that year and even two more over the summer to graduate on time. But I learned an invaluable lesson (not for the last time): know where you're going, and keep your eyes on the prize.

Goal-Shaped Plans

Dwight D. Eisenhower rose to prominence and the presidency perhaps more because of his skills with logistics than any other reason. He understood the many steps of minutiae needed to reach a goal. His most famous triumph came from overseeing the logistics of the D-Day invasion. "Plans are nothing; the planning is everything," he would say.[3] He knew how to adjust on the fly. But he also knew that if you don't have a goal, then you're not adjusting; you're flailing.

If you don't have a stable identity goal—a vision of who you should be—you'll never get any closer. You won't be planning; you'll be reacting. You'll be hoping to spasm in the right direction. At best, you'll be doing the next thing because it's there, with no idea whether it gets you closer to the goal. For Christians, our identity goal is clear—it's Jesus. But following an identity path of imitation will prove more countercultural than you might think.

Imitation or Self-Creation?

What's the best way to become who you want to be? I think the answer is to use a model. If you want to be a world-class swimmer, watch Michael Phelps and Katie Ledecky. If your goal is to write murder mysteries, read Conan Doyle and Agatha Christie.

This might sound obvious, but it's not! There's a major cultural push currently against using any kind of model in your identity formation.[4]

Philosophers call this new view on identity "expressive individualism." The idea is that you, and you alone, need to decide and shape who you are. Don't let anybody else interfere. "You are who you feel yourself to be on the inside and acting in accordance with this identity constitutes living authentically."[5] In expressive individualism, you are completely unique, which means there's nothing out there for you to imitate. You discover the ideal of your identity through a deep dive within, where you look for the buried treasure of the blueprints of you. When you find them, you'll know your identity goal! But no one can tell you where these blueprints are or how to find them. It's doubtful whether anyone besides you can even read them if you do find them.

Imitating the Ideal

I want to go back to an old idea that will explain why our modern vision of identity feels so much more challenging today than in the past. For at least two thousand years, people followed Plato's vision for how identity and the world works. It's called the Theory of Forms. Basically, the idea is that somewhere out there, in the fabric of the universe, there is an ideal "form" of everything that people instinctively know.

The chair was Plato's famous example. There's one perfect, ideal chair that's just "out there." When you peruse IKEA, you recognize a chair because of its "chairness," even though it's not *the* perfect chair. Same with dogs or sports cars. You recognize dogs by their "doggyness" and so on. Forms give us categories and a shared vision of what's beautiful. Each individual chair, though not perfect, is someone's best approximation of the ideal form. These forms explain the gap between the way things are and the way we all feel they *ought* to be.[6]

This Theory of Forms also applies to human identity. There is some ideal form of the human being—the perfect man or woman. According to Plato's thought, it's out there, as surely as the rule of gravity, even if we can't see it. What we *do* see are human models who, as with the chair analogy, do a better or worse job of matching up to the ideal. Their heroism or villainy is plain to all because we all know, inherently, the ideal. Our goal as human beings is like the goal of any craftsman: to imitate what's ideal. We strive to gain a clearer mental picture of this ideal man or woman. Then we set about honing our craft: perfecting our skills in order to approximate this ideal form.

In your identity craftsmanship, your product (your identity) will not look exactly like any others. It will come with all the marks of your own artistic style. And you will fall short of replicating the ideal. No one achieves their ideal self. But people influenced by Plato's Theory of Forms believed you could make objective progress in imitating an ideal form, whether in crafting a chair or your identity. And you could critique other people's work as getting close to or falling short of these inherently understood ideal forms.

This philosophy produced ancient therapies, like Stoicism. You sit down with your Stoic therapist, feeling depressed and anxious. Your therapist, Zeno, explains to you what's happening. "Your feelings are out of sync with the ideal. You expect the world to be other than it is, and that's why you're unhappy. Observe better. Look a little more closely," Zeno advises. "Adjust your thinking and emotions in order to better imitate the true form of this world."

I'm spending so much time on Plato and his Theory of Forms because he was onto something our world has largely left behind when talking about identity. Historically, your identity project was to imitate a fixed ideal out there in the world. Now, in expressive individualism, it's about making the world out there conform to your ideal within. In case you're wondering, that's quite a bit harder.

Being Transformed into... You

Overall, the Theory of Forms is a lot closer to the truth than expressive individualism. There is an ideal form of human identity out there—it's Jesus. We also all grow through imitation. We need models. It's not that you don't do any creative self-expressing along the way; it's just that no human being made him- or herself from scratch. Ever. Adam and Eve were created in the image of God, and that's who they were supposed to imitate (Genesis 1:26-27). Even without sin, in the perfect Garden of Eden, God wanted them to grow more fully into their identity in imitating his creating and sustaining work (Genesis 1:28).

So what is your identity goal? Most Christians get that it's looking like and following Jesus—that you should "find your identity in Christ." That sounds great, but what does it look like exactly? The Bible says a lot about who God is and how he wants us to live. But 2 Corinthians 3:18 offers a concise formula for identity growth:

> *We all, with unveiled face, beholding the glory of the Lord, are being transformed into the same image from one degree of glory to another.*

This verse works like the coding that runs underneath the ideal human development software. If you're a Christian, then God is constantly transforming you into the image of Jesus, including every part of your identity. But you're a finite human being, so you're never going to be Jesus. So what's the identity end point for you? The world might call it your "best self," but you could call it your "Jesus-self": the version of you that is more and more like him.

> *If anyone is in Christ, he* **is** *a new creation. The old has passed away; behold, the new has come.*
>
> *(2 Corinthians 5:17)*

As a Christian, you already *are* new, but you're also *becoming* something new. We're told to "seek the things that are above, where Christ is" (Colossians 3:1). Seek, rather than *find*. Seeking is an active job. It means you're not there yet. You experience both being and becoming.

This should give you some stable ground under your feet. Christian identity transformation is not one of those body-switch comedies where the fifteen-year-old girl wakes up living in the skin of her menopausal mother. You won't feel an out-of-placeness with your transformed self. You're still you, and the transformation is happening gradually.

But an identity goal of imitating Jesus more closely should also give you hope and purpose. You're not stuck. Your identity is not boxed in. With your new "Jesus-self," the best is always yet to come. You're becoming more who you are and were always meant to be.

Foal to Stallion

The second-century Church Father Irenaeus said that the glory of God is a human being fully alive.[7] We glorify God by growing into the fullness of who we were made to be. This is God's main project in you as well as yours.

The Christian identity goal of becoming who you are might sound abstract. But we see examples of this sort of thing all the time. A male horse, when he's born, is called a foal. You've seen the footage, or maybe you've been on the farm. His knobby little knees shake as he struggles to get standing; then his legs splay, and he tumbles back on the ground. After much effort, he stands upright. He walks a few unsteady paces before collapsing again.

In the next four and a half years, this horse will go through three more stages of development: yearling (1-2 years old), colt (under 4), and stallion (4+ years old). When you think of a horse, or when you see one in a picture book, which stage do you imagine? Probably the stallion. Between a foal and a stallion, is there any debate which one is more glorious? Which one is more of what a horse *should* look like? The stallion is the fullest, most beautiful version. It is a horse "most fully alive." Yet when the foal is born, what animal would you call him? Would you classify him as anything but a horse? Of course not. Over the years, he is becoming more of who he already is.

Beholding

When you put your faith in Jesus, God gives you a remade core identity (2 Corinthians 5:17). For the rest of your life, you will become more of who you are. But you have a choice: you can run joyfully toward this every day, or you can squat back on your hind legs like a dog insistent on smelling mystery pavement muck, making God choke-drag you home.

How do you work with God to get closer to your goal faster? 2 Corinthians 3:18 says, "We all, with unveiled face, *beholding* the glory of the Lord, are being transformed."

Beholding transforms us. What does that mean? Most of us don't do much beholding these days. You don't behold a gas station. You certainly don't behold the internet. You might behold something at an art gala—if you ever go to those.

But we need to get better at beholding because it's the key. We have to behold the glory of the Lord in the person of Jesus.

Beholding implies a personal, concrete, and experiential act. When you behold something, you're engaging more senses more fully than as a passive listener or observer.[8] In a sense I'm talking about reading the Bible, listening to sermons, and prayer—but the crucial thing is that you use these things to not just know about the person of God but really behold him.[9] You engage the inner eye of your soul.

Beholding Jesus is an ongoing process. You don't look at Jesus once and then figure, "Okay, I've got this now." That would be like getting on a bike, looking at the stop sign at the end of a long road, and then closing your eyes while you pedal there.

Beholding Jesus

Oprah helped popularize vision boards and manifesting. Manifesting is the idea that if you have a clear vision of a future reality for yourself (like cruising on your future boat at your future lake house) and you keep focusing on that vision, you will manifest it into reality. It's become sadly popular because it exploits for selfish gain the way that God has made our identity—you become what you behold.

Manifesting is a secular, corrupted version of the spiritual exercise of beholding. Beholding means worshiping. You envision something, some reality you love and desire. You keep it in front of your mind's eye. As you behold that thing, you will drift toward it naturally. It pulls you along. It's the tide of your soul.

Manifesting a new career might indeed lead you to one because you're focusing your desire on that thing and it's transforming how you live. But you'll find yourself no happier when you get it because you're worshiping the wrong thing. The challenge, then, is *what* you behold (or worship). It's fixing your mind—not on some bedazzled version of yourself, decked out with awards and vacation homes, but on Jesus. It's keeping your mind and heart on how glorious he is. As you do that, you'll move closer to the goal. The real you, the more Jesus-like version of you, will keep emerging.

Mainly, It's Passive

"Being transformed into the same image," "beholding the glory of the Lord," "becoming who you are"—maybe it all still sounds a bit abstract. What exactly should I be *doing*? That's part of both the gift and frustration of God's identity project. Mainly, it's passive. "We all ... beholding the glory of the Lord, *are being* transformed" (2 Corinthians 3:18). That means you're not the one doing the transforming. God does that. It happens gradually, invisibly, internally.

As you think about the previous ten years of your life, or the next ten, they are mostly filled with just doing the things you need to do. That's fine. You're not missing something. If you're beholding Jesus, a specific decision isn't likely to take you off course or cause you to lose your identity goal, because your identity transformation is primarily passive. It's happening all the time under the surface—not because of something you do or some role you have but because of what you are beholding. Remember your "master identity" from the last chapter? It's really formed by what you love. And what you love is what you behold. And what you behold will shape you. It will shape who you spend time with, what you do, what you say, and how you say it. It will inform all your other identities.

Take six-year-old Rosie. She grows up beholding her mom, whom she loves. Every day, Rosie is transforming more into herself. She'll also look more like her mom, in her own way. She's learning and developing constantly but almost never consciously. She doesn't wake up thinking, "Today, as I watch my mom, I'll learn some new words, become more optimistic, and develop a passion for biking." She becomes as she beholds.

More of Your Jesus-Self

A Christian's identity project brings together our longings for stability, growth, and purpose. You are transforming, but you're not losing your true self. This can be a big concern for a Christian looking at the road ahead. It was for me. At one point, I felt Jesus calling me to go after him more, but I hesitated. Many of the models of "serious" Christians I saw were not anything I wanted to imitate. But God is not transforming you into Brandon, the seminary student who prescribes you a new book in every conversation, or into Megan, who makes her own soap from scratch and labels it with Bible verses. (Not unless that's who you are already!) Jesus won't do violence to the specific ways he made you in God's image to begin with. Odds are, God doesn't have a plane waiting to take you to Africa at the end of your next ten years' journey. Where God wants to take you is to an identity that looks more like Jesus and more like you.

You will become something new—have no doubt about that. But this is rarely about externals, like a new job or new city. Jesus transforms your inner self—so it's more about how engaged you are with his purposes in whichever context you're in.

Let's take an example. One of the fruits of the Spirit is gentleness (Galatians 5:22-23). None of the fruits are optional—you will and must become more gentle. Jesus will stamp every one of the fruits of his Spirit deeper into you as you keep beholding him. Now, God has endowed certain people, through nature and nurture, with more of a spirit of gentleness to begin with. You may or may not be one of them. But Jesus is gentle. He wills for every Christian to grow in that way. This means that one thing you can know for sure that you're moving toward in the next ten years is gentleness. That does *not* mean that if you go after your identity goal, you'll end up morphing into Mr. Rogers.

A Christian first-grade teacher and a Christian NFL coach will both grow in the gentleness modeled by Jesus. But it will look different. The first-grade teacher hopefully will have to do less dialing back on expletives. The NFL coach will still give less runway for meltdowns over shoelace-tying. Both are becoming more of who they are in Jesus, but both will make progress in gentleness in ways that are authentic to their personality and context. They will still use consequences, but there'll be less yelling. They will still have expectations but less cynicism. Gentleness won't feel forced. It won't feel like play-acting. It will follow naturally from beholding Jesus as someone who is gentle toward *them*. Jesus will reveal his gentleness to the teacher and the coach personally, specifically, and proportionally—as one of his many good traits.

Paul uses the same "transform" verb of 2 Corinthians 3:18 in only a handful of other places. One is Romans 12:2:

> *Do not be conformed to this world, but* ***be transformed*** *by the renewal of your mind.*

This is how you get transformed into your Jesus-self. Your renewal happens internally, in your mind and heart, then radiates out in your words and actions. You behold how Jesus treats you gently. It changes how you think about the world. Life doesn't need to be harsh and unforgiving. You can handle people with respect even when they're way out of line. Jesus has given you a new spirit, which includes infinite gentleness. As you keep looking at the goal of Jesus, you'll naturally go toward it, becoming more of your best self along the way.

Questions for Discussion and Reflection

1. Who are the people you want to imitate? What ideals have they captured, and why do you want to imitate those traits?
2. What are some ways you have been transformed into a better version of yourself? How do you hope that will happen in the future?
3. What aspect of Jesus would you like to behold and become better? Is there a verse or passage that shows that?

CHAPTER 3

Making the Best of What You're Given

When I was growing up, my parents would occasionally talk to me and my brother about our personalities. My mom told me several times that I had a reflective spirit. She noticed that I liked to withdraw and make up stories by myself. But neither of my parents ever used the words extroverted or introverted. So, I was at a loss one Sunday morning, when I was sitting in my eighth-grade Sunday-school class and the teacher asked us each to share which of the two we were.

After listening closely to the descriptions, I decided that, from what I had heard from my parents and felt was mostly true, I was introverted. At that point, a cute, extroverted girl in my class interjected, "There's no way you're introverted, Justin! You love talking to people!" Enough said. Clearly I was mistaken. I was most *definitely* extroverted.

My mom was not convinced. But what did she know? For the next seventeen years, I self-identified in every test and conversation as an extrovert. After all, I *did* enjoy people. I enjoyed talking. Most particularly, I enjoyed being *seen* as extroverted because, whatever that meant, it was good. It meant other people would want to be around me. They would see me as a source of energy—the life of the party.

I remember many times when I leaned hard into this identity. In social gatherings, I would kick myself up into my loudest, most gregarious self. It wasn't as if that person wasn't me—as if I was trying to play-act as somebody else. It's just that I was playing into one *side* of myself—one particular expression of my identity that I kept trying to double down on and strengthen. And it worked. As I developed "extroverted Justin," I learned to hurtle past social inertia and signal affability.

It took until my first year of marriage for me to rethink this side of my identity. When I told my wife I was extroverted, she laughed. "You *love* being by yourself so you can read or write. That's how you recharge. You're definitely an introvert." She and my mom were right. I had not only been fooling others, but I had also successfully fooled myself for nearly twenty years about one of the most basic elements of my personality.

Truth is, we aren't that good at knowing who we are. We deceive ourselves. We tell slanted stories. We reconstruct reality. We are simultaneously too harsh and too lenient on ourselves. Our inner world changes so rapidly that it's hard to see the bigger picture.

If you want to become who you truly are supposed to be, you need Jesus. You also need others. You need an outside perspective. What are you really working with—what identities are you holding? What should you *do* with all those possible versions of yourself? You need God and other people to help you see yourself truly. Then you can start moving toward your Jesus-self.

Givenness: You Can't Escape Yourself

As we saw in chapter one, your identity is your sense of self that connects who you are as a product of your past with who you wish to be in the future. A large portion of your sense of self comes from who you are as a product of your past. This comes partly from your identities of origin but also includes roles given to you or affinities you are naturally inclined to. Your identity has been shaped by people and circumstances entirely outside of your control. These are what we'll call your *givens*.

Think about how much of your life is a given. Take just your genetics. The color of your skin and your eyes, your height, your predisposition to diabetes or depression, and how fast you can run are all givens that were thrust upon you without the slightest consideration of your preferences. As influential as parents and genetics are, your givens don't stop there. The timing of your birth, your siblings, your nationality, and your home are all given to you, no questions asked.

What You Do with Your Givens

Even so, you still choose what to do with all those givens. How do you understand yourself as a product of your past, and then connect that with who you wish to be in the future? There are some givens you will push against, and others you will want to embrace.

Let's consider personality tests. They are about discovering givenness. You have givens about your temperament. You're predisposed to look at and approach life through a given lens. Those things are part of your being. But personality tests neglect the fact that you're also becoming.

If your personality test has the final say-so in your life, it becomes a prison. Some people develop a victimhood mentality because they make this mistake. *This is who I am. These are the cards that I was dealt. I don't really have a choice in what I do or how I respond.* If you let the givens in your life hold that kind of power, then all anyone else can do is accept and adapt to who you are, even if who you are is a pompous jerk.

My family used to talk about personalities in terms of Winnie the Pooh characters. One of the main characters in Winnie the Pooh is Tigger.[10] He has boundless energy; he's also impulsive, competitive, risk-taking, and sociable. Those are givens. Those are ways that Tigger will naturally express himself—ways that will never come naturally to Eeyore, the depressed donkey. One day, Tigger is bouncing at full speed towards Pooh's house. On his way, he crashes into Eeyore, who is gazing despondently at his reflection, knocking Eeyore into the river.

After Tigger fishes Eeyore out of the water, how should the two of them reconcile? On the one hand, it's not fair for Eeyore to question Tigger: "Why do you need to bounce? After all, I (Eeyore) never do." Bouncing is what Tigger does. That's a given. But on the other hand, Tigger should not complain, "Eeyore, why didn't you move? After all, Tiggers need to bounce. Everyone should know that and clear out of my way."

To reconcile, they will conclude that Tigger should indeed keep bouncing but do so more carefully. He should watch where he's bouncing and control that part of his personality out of respect for others.

It's the same for you. Your personality (like any given) is not a fatalistic determination of the rest of your life. You're still on the hook to decide how you let a given in your life affect you.

Some givens in your life you should celebrate (e.g. having loving parents), others you should try to overcome (being prone to jealousy), and others you will need to cope with (your poor memory). You will make a terrible hash of your life if you misjudge which one is which: if you decide, for instance, that everyone should celebrate your poor memory. Just because something about you is a given doesn't automatically make it good or bad. You need wisdom to discern how to respond to each given.

The difficulty is that the decision of what you do with your givens is itself influenced by givens. Tim Keller, the late renowned pastor of Redeemer NYC, had a great example of this. Take a young man who feels both violent rage and homosexual desires. Place this same man among ninth-century Nordic barbarians and among twenty-first-century New Yorkers. He will likely cultivate one desire and repress the other depending on which society he's in, each of which praises one set of values and frowns on the other.[11]

This means you need something better (and wiser) than culture or social media to discern how to respond to your givens.

You Don't Know Yourself As Well As You Think

The shifting winds of culture are not the only obstacle to becoming your best self. Probably the biggest one is your own mind and heart. When you are the only one to whom you'll listen on the subject of your identity, your judgments will get out of whack! Jeremiah 17:9 says, "The heart is deceitful above all things, and desperately sick; who can understand it?" This means that not only are your self-evaluations untrustworthy, but you can't even be entirely sure *why* they're untrustworthy. Our hearts are slippery and deceptive—most especially when it comes to *why* we do the things we do. Your heart has a vested interest in keeping safe its little comforts and securities, and will deflect your self-examinations like an addict.

Oftentimes we don't think how we should or want what we should. "There is a way that seems right to a man, but its end is the way to death" (Proverbs 16:25). This verse is a sobering reminder that you can be fully convinced of the rightness of your opinions and decisions, but all that means is that you are fully self-deceived on your pathway to death.

My example at the beginning of self-identifying as an extrovert is a relatively innocuous one. The skills and habits I pursued in order to cultivate that side of myself were, on the whole, useful. But let's say that I identify as a moody artist of unrecognized genius. Judging from more than a few examples, that means I should dress in eclectic fashion, speak condescendingly, and acquire a drinking problem. Over the years, I will be developing this self—I'm growing, in a manner of speaking, but that "growth" is not progress. My heart has conceived a vision of my future self that is not ideal. I should never have developed in that direction at all. I am being "true to myself," but it is a bad self. And there are worse examples of "self-development" you could think of.

You can see why I'm arguing that we need Jesus to guide us through the labyrinth of our selves. Bible teacher

Paul E. Miller explains this as our need for Jesus as our Good Shepherd:

> *Without the Shepherd guiding us to see our true selves in relationship to him, we can lose our way and become obsessed with self. Instead of seeing our bent toward evil, we can become increasingly touchy, supersensitive to self but insensitive to others. We no longer see ourselves clearly.*[12]

The One Who Knows You Best

We need to lean on God and the people he's put around us to test hypotheses about ourselves. The book of Job takes us inside a conversation where God confronts Job (and us) with just how little he knows about why God has set certain givens in place. God asks Job if he knows how the world was made (Job 38:4), whether Job sketched the constellations up in the sky (v 31-33), and whether he's watching when a baby mountain goat is born (39:1-4). Line after line, verse after verse, God reminds Job of the beautiful, fearful, and stunningly complex givens that surround him things Job has probably never given more than a few minutes' thought to. To his credit, Job gets the point: "Behold, I am of small account; what shall I answer you? I lay my hand on my mouth" (40:4).

Out of all the givens that make up your struggles, your background, your giftings and deficiencies, and your environment, there are some that you do not like and would not have chosen. But if there's anyone you can trust to tell you what to do with those givens, and how to become your best self, it's the God who created all those givens in the first place.

Enjoy the Givens You Can't Change

You didn't create yourself. God did. God's plan is for us to always be discovering ourselves (becoming) in the midst of our givens (I Corinthians 9:19-22). When circumstances and relationships change in ways that you can't control, you discover afresh how to live out who you are meant to be. "Let each person lead the life that the Lord has assigned to him" (7:17). Coming to appreciate the givenness of your life shouldn't be a cause of frustration but of humility and gratitude.

You were born into a world, a family, an ethnicity, a nationality, a history, and a society that you had no part in deciding but which exerts tremendous force on shaping every aspect of your life. When you accept those things as givens from the Lord, it brings a good deal of peace and self-acceptance. You understand that "accepting yourself" really has a lot more to do with accepting God, the world that he's made, and how he's created you.

This can help us even when we are frustrated and feeling that life doesn't make sense. The apostle Paul was able to write:

> *I have learned, in whatever situation I am, to be content. I know how to be brought low, and I know how to abound ... I have learned the secret of facing plenty and hunger, abundance and need. I can do all things through him who strengthens me. (Philippians 4:11-13)*

It's funny—a lot of people snag that last sentence as a motivational slogan proclaiming that God will give them the strength to do whatever they set their mind to. But its meaning is almost the exact opposite. Paul's secret is his recognition that God decides the givens of his life. Whatever those givens are, he can use them in service of his one goal: growing into his true identity, which is to look more like Jesus (Philippians 3:10-14).

Helpful as it is to be at peace with our givens, we still need to make choices about how we live our lives and which identities we prioritize. How can we accept the givens of our life (being) while growing into the best version of ourselves that is shaped by those givens (becoming)?

Let's take a well-known biblical figure as a case study: King David. We'll look at three key identities (one of origin, one of role, and one of affinity) that shaped David's life. We're going to see what happened to his givens when he focused his life on the Lord—and also what happened when he failed to do so. The goal is to start to see what it looks like to have an identity centered on the Lord Jesus.

David the Shepherd: An Identity of Origin

We meet David in his mid to late teens as a shepherd (1 Samuel 16:11). Being a shepherd was a given in David's background, part of his "being." He never leaves behind this identity of origin.

But David's shepherd identity gains new power as he keeps connecting it to his relationship with God. When he offers to fight Goliath, he explains why the decision feels natural:

> *Your servant used to keep sheep for his father. And when there came a lion, or a bear, and took a lamb from the flock, I went after him and struck him and delivered it out of his mouth. And if he arose against me, I caught him by his beard and struck him and killed him. Your servant has struck down both lions and bears, and this*

> *uncircumcised Philistine shall be like one of them, for he has defied the armies of the living God.*
>
> *(1 Samuel 17:34-36)*

Goliath is the bear attacking the flock of God's people. David's ready to do what a good shepherd does—what he's always done. He kills the enemy, saves the flock, and becomes Israel's shepherd-hero.

What does it look like for you to take your identities of origin and use them in God's service? Maybe your parents immigrated to the US from Eastern Europe, or you moved around a lot as a kid. Being a newcomer and the process of assimilation is part of your identity of origin. As you behold Jesus, who welcomed you when you were estranged from God, you develop a heart for the outsider. You welcome others. You understand more fully that living the Christian life is a kind of exile (1 Peter 2:11), so you work to strengthen those who feel they're living on the margins and help them look forward to their eternal home.

Much later in his life, David goes majorly off track. He commits adultery and murder. God sends Nathan the prophet to take David to task—and how does Nathan cut to David's heart? He tells him a story about a sheep (2 Samuel 12). There was a poor man who loved his one lamb. He carried it around and shared his food and water with it, like the half-adorable, half-revolting way a woman lets her purse dog take sips from her glass. But then his rich neighbor has a guest over, and rather than using a sheep from his own giant flock, he takes the poor man's lamb and slaughters it for his dinner. When Nathan finishes up this story, he does the big reveal—that David is the ruthless rich guy. All at once, David's mask falls off.

He sees himself clearly. The sheep story makes him realize that he's betrayed his given shepherd identity.

Most importantly, as David grows in his shepherd identity, he comes to know the Lord as the Shepherd. Only someone so intimately acquainted with the shepherd life—the tranquility of green pastures and still waters and the fear of the dark valley—could pen perhaps the most famous chapter in the Bible, Psalm 23. "The LORD is *my* shepherd" (Psalm 23:1). This spiritual revelation had been growing in David's mind since he was a child.

In many ways, David's shepherd identity is the bedrock of his life. But it also becomes one of the keys to his relationship with God. What is David called to do? To be a shepherd to the people of Israel, under the greater Shepherd, Jesus.

God uses your identities to teach you as well—most importantly, to teach you about himself. For example, if you grew up in a house full of music and then became a musician, God will use this to teach you about him. How is music meant to glorify God and connect us with his story of redemption? Why does God use music and song as an eternal way of worshiping him (Revelation 15:3-4)? How can music serve to bring a whole person—body, soul, and spirit—into fuller enjoyment of God?

What do you think God wants to show you about himself through your identities of origin?

David the King: An Identity of Role

David is probably around seventeen when Samuel anoints him king over Israel (1 Samuel 16:1-13). It takes roughly another twenty years for David to actually get to the throne in Jerusalem with all of Israel officially recognizing him as king. That means David lives for twenty years *knowing* this part of his identity (kingship) but not seeing it actualized. At seventeen, he is king. That's now a stable part of his being. Yet in the next twenty years, he does a lot of *becoming* a king.

There's a period of several years in David's early to mid-twenties when he's on the run. He's camping in the desert and hiding out in caves as Saul tries to kill him. He witnesses betrayal and the slaughter of innocent people on his account (1 Samuel 22:6-23). He barely escapes from an enemy king by pretending to be crazy and drooling all over himself (21:10-15). He saves a city from destruction only to have them turn around and sell him out (23:1-14).

He can't have felt very kingly during these years. Where were the purple pillows? The goblets and celebrity cameos? Yet slowly and surely, in the midst of all these troubles, a trickle of followers found their way to David. "Everyone who was in distress, and everyone who was in debt, and everyone who was bitter in soul, gathered to him" (1 Samuel 22:2). Sounds a lot like the type of people who found their way to King Jesus.

Just like David, maybe there are things God is calling you to that you don't see the final evidence of yet. You're applying to jobs, but no doors seem to be opening. You long to have children, but you still haven't conceived. You're working hard as a volunteer in your community but see no impact.

David's story can reassure you that even (and often especially) when you feel like you're not living your best life, God is at work. David focused on what he knew was right, not on becoming the king he knew God had chosen him to be. Then God used that very faithfulness to turn David into exactly the king that God meant for David to become.

You and I are called to pursue faithfulness in the process of becoming. What does faithfulness look like in your life? Are you grinding out a degree while you long to be in your field making a difference? Make a difference in your schoolwork—in your diligence on your assignment today. Soak in the best that your teachers have to offer and give your best support to your classmates around you.

Are you watching friends live out full lives in relationships or with families, while you feel like singlehood puts you on the sidelines? Faithfully maximize the opportunities and freedoms you enjoy to live out your identity in a way that serves God's kingdom. Use the specific challenges of singleness to deepen and solidify your relationship with God, which will forever take precedence over every other.

David the Soldier

Some people are good fighters, and David was one of them. He loved the battle; that was a given part of his being—an identity of affinity. Of course, God was the one who gave David victory against Goliath and others, but he used David's given skills—training, audacity, and quick thinking—to do it.

This part of his identity also grows. David the boy grabbing lions by the beard (1 Samuel 17:35) becomes David the four-star general defeating a massive army (2 Samuel 10:18). He never stops winning. David's affinity for battle and conquest evolves throughout his life.

Interestingly, it's his *neglect* of this identity that brings about his worst fall. "In the spring of the year, the time when kings go out to battle, David sent Joab, and his servants with him ... But David remained at Jerusalem" (2 Samuel 11:1). David is lounging instead of fighting. Then he notices a beautiful woman. She turns out to be the wife of one of his soldiers who's fighting in the battle that David should be leading. David descends into adultery and murder. In other words, David's denial of his identity as a warrior-king led to his fall. Success made him believe that this part of his identity was now beneath him or at least optional.

Your given affinities—your passions, skills, and interests—are powerful tools that God will use to shape you as you use them to shape your environment. A good affinity will mature throughout your life, like a spreading tree. If your relationship with God remains your master identity, it will grow and redirect these affinities so that they bear fruit in every season of your life. (See Psalm 1:3.)

Neglecting one of your gifts or affinities does not necessarily dump you into sin, but you have gifts for a reason. "Whoever is slack in his work is a brother to him who destroys" (Proverbs 18:9). God's word warns against an indulgent idleness that destroys you and your opportunities for good:

> *Having gifts that differ according to the grace given to us, let us use them: if prophecy, in proportion to our faith, if service, in our serving, the one who teaches, in his teaching; the one who exhorts, in his exhortation; the one who contributes, in generosity; the one who leads, with zeal; the one who does acts of mercy, with cheerfulness.*
>
> *(Romans 12:6-8)*

On the other hand, don't mistake your affinities for the end goal.

As he matures, David comes to see that the ultimate goal in a battle is not victory in itself but rather the peace and enjoyment of God that victory brings. This means David's real battle is over his heart (Psalm 51). He longs for a more peaceful, reflective life that is connected with God: "One thing I have asked of the LORD, that will I seek after: that I may dwell in the house of the LORD all the days of my life, to gaze upon the beauty of the LORD and to inquire in his temple" (Psalm 27:4). David learns that his given affinity for battle will not bring the fulfillment he wants by itself. David's master identity of his relationship with God is what he's battling *for*. He has a higher affinity—the desire to live in peaceful enjoyment of God.

You can assess the value and direction of your affinities and gifts by holding them up against the end goal of looking like Jesus. Is your pursuit of business savvy and making lots of money bringing you closer to that image? There are ways that it will and ways that it will not. Is it to make you look good or to honor God? God wires you with particular gifts and interests to bring him glory in your particular way.

You, along with David and every other person in the world, are both being and becoming through the givens of your life. God wants you to grow in understanding and using your givens to become your Jesus-self—the version of yourself that displays how great God is. He wants to take you on that path. Ask him to show you what your givens are and how to use them to become more fully who you already are in Jesus.

Where We've Been and Where We're Going

Let me wrap up the main ideas we've covered so far. Your identity is your sense of self that connects who you are as a product of the past with who you wish to be in the future. This is complicated because you have many sub-identities that come from your origins, your roles, and your affinities. In chapter 2, we learned God's goal for our identity as Christians: to look more like Jesus. This happens by beholding Jesus. As you see more clearly who Jesus is, you grow more fully into your best self. We also gained perspective on how much of our identity is given to us, yet we still have decisions about what to do with those givens.

In the next section, we'll look at three practical ways that beholding Jesus shows up in our identity journey, and how they both align with and contradict our world's vision of identity construction. You're called to live authentically, to live free, and to tell yourself (and others) the real story of who you are and who you're becoming.

Questions for Discussion and Reflection

1. What's a given in your life you can celebrate? What's a given in your life you wish wasn't there?
2. What's one of your identities of origin? How can you see the value of that? How is God teaching you through it?
3. What's one of your identities of role right now? How can you see more value in that and use it for Jesus?
4. What one of your identities of affinity? What might it look like to develop that affinity for Jesus' sake, not yours?

CHAPTER 4

Being Authentic

There's almost nothing more endearing than authenticity. We love the celebrity who's not afraid to show their quirky side, the politician who uses plain talk, or the small-town hero who remembers her roots. No pretending, no deceit, just raw authenticity. But "authentic" is a dangerous word. For starters, it presumes you know who you're supposed to be. You've got it all figured out—it's just a matter of having the courage to stay true to yourself. But as we've already seen, you are always changing as you move towards who you want to be. Your identity is your sense of self that connects who you are as a product of your past with who you wish to be in the future. It's not just being; it's becoming. And if your self is always changing, then what does it mean to be true to yourself?

The second problem you run into in pursuing authenticity comes as soon as you realize that you're doing things you don't like. You snapped at your brother, and you can't understand why you did that—he didn't deserve it. Suddenly, you've got two versions of yourself that are in conflict. Which one is the authentic you—the person who snapped or the person who wishes she hadn't?

We live in this authenticity paradox: you want to be yourself, but then again there are parts of you that you wish were different and parts of you that are always changing. This is precisely where the biblical categories of an old self and a new self come in handy (as we're about to discover). They help sort through which self to be true to.

When you're a Christian, there is a sense in which you *do* have a good heart. But there's another sense in which you *really* are a bad person. If we are going to become more like Jesus, the first thing we need to do is see that we are people at war with ourselves. We have multiple selves that are in conflict.

> *[You were taught] to put off your old self, which belongs to your former manner of life and is corrupt through deceitful desires, and to be renewed in the spirits of your minds, and to put on the new self, created after the likeness of God in true righteousness and holiness.*
> *(Ephesians 4:22-24)*

You have an old self, which is "corrupt through deceitful desires," and a new self, which is "created after the likeness of God." But look closely at the actions the Bible calls for. It's not merely about trading good atomic habits for bad ones. It's calling you to put off an entire self. Our selves, before Jesus, were corrupt; with him, though, we have a new, renewed self.

That might sound a bit extreme. Politicians can be corrupt. Corporate lawyers can be corrupt. Me—I just need to focus a little more. The whole self-help field is built on the premise that, mostly, you're okay. You just need to practice self-acceptance and tap into your inner strength. But the Christian view of things is that in order to get to sanctification (becoming your best self by becoming like Jesus), you need to first take the uncomfortable step of killing off your old, corrupt self.

It is at the same time an unpleasant and a cathartic process.

"I Am Okay"

Before we get into how the Bible solves the problem of our own wrongdoing, let's look at another proposed solution. Here's how the twentieth-century identity pioneer Virginia Satir tried to deal with it in her "Declaration of Self-Esteem":

> *Everything that comes out of me is authentically mine because I alone chose it ... However I look and sound, whatever I say and do, and whatever I think and feel at a given moment in time is me. This is authentic and represents where I am in that moment in time. When I review later how I looked and sounded, what I said and did, and how I thought and felt, some parts may turn out to be unfitting. I can discard that which is unfitting, and keep that which proved fitting, and invent something new for that which I discarded ... I own me, and therefore I can engineer me. I am me and I am okay.*

"Unfitting" is about the softest, squishiest way you could possibly acknowledge that you do and say some really bad stuff. Her description of identity formation makes it sound like you're trying on a pair of pants. Do you like the way they fit? Maybe they're a little baggy, or the color isn't your first choice, or the pockets aren't in quite the right place. But ultimately, if you're happy enough with how they fit, that's all that matters. And you're the only one who can decide this.

Satir also has a relaxed way of talking about what it's like to "discard that which is unfitting." Apparently, it's that easy—just like taking off one pair of pants and trying on another. "I can engineer me," she asserts. As if it were that simple. Just engineer a version of your self who stops losing your patience or having one more drink.

Contrast Satir's vision of our authentic self with the Bible's brutally honest one:

> *I do not understand my own actions. For I do not do what I want, but I do the very thing I hate ... I know that nothing good dwells within me, that is, in my flesh. For I have the desire to do what is right, but not the ability to carry it out. For I do not do the good I want, but the evil I do not want is what I keep on doing. (Romans 7:15-20)*[13]

Judge for yourself which description gets to a deeper truth.

Satir's depiction of our ideal self is aiming at self-esteem. The Bible's statement aims at something much greater. The writer, Paul, is telling the whole tragic story of a broken humanity—of a fallen greatness within all of us that has brought identity disillusionment ever since Adam and Eve first rebelled. You are capable of envisioning a great version of your self—wide-hearted and expansive with love and charity and self-control. Then you're confronted with the real version of your self. It's not that. How could it ever *be* that?

If you aim for self-esteem but cut God and sin out of the picture, you will make peace with the mold and dry rot in the structure of your self because you refuse to call sin what it is. You will underestimate the ferocity of your identity turmoil because you don't want to believe that your authentic self is really that bad. That's why you'll often hear a celebrity, when some atrocity is exposed, say afterward, "I don't know how that happened. That wasn't really me."

The truth is, you really *are* that person. You are the person who spread rumors, flipped out at their kids, or drank way too much. It's not just a blip. It's not just a bad hair day. You have an authentic self (in the sense of real and true) that really is that bad. And on your own, you can't do much about it. "I can engineer me" will only get you so far, especially if all your engineering amounts to is reflecting from time to time on what didn't quite *fit*. Sure, you can work on yourself, but Paul's agonized statement will remain true: "I have the desire to do what is right, but not the ability to carry it out" (v 18).

Satir's conclusion at the bottom of her declaration of self-esteem proves the hollowness of her philosophy. She says: "I am me and I am okay." Really? Everything you've said, everything you've done, everything you've wanted is just... okay?

Well, yes, you may be thinking, *because the alternative is too bleak*. If it comes down to a choice of stuffing sin under the carpet or seeing your self as morally bankrupt, who would pick the latter? You'd only want to see yourself the way Paul describes if you believed you could change those ugly parts of you completely. But this is the crucial point: it is possible. There's a new self as well as an old self. And the new self is beautiful.

You Should Both Hate and Love Your Self

Consider again the plain-speaking honesty of the Bible when it comes to the problems in your identity: "I do not do what I want, but I do the very thing I *hate*" (v 15). This is no longer dealing in the realm of fitting and unfitting, but right and wrong, love and hate. There are parts of your authentic self that are objectively bad.

But alongside this painful truth, the Bible provides a different vision of the authentic self, which gives you hope: "Now if I do what I do not want, it is no longer *I* who do it, but *sin* that dwells within me" (v 20). When you're a Christian, there is a version of you that doesn't consent—doesn't even *do*—all that stuff that you end up hating. And that version is also your true self.

That carries a different nuance from the celebrity apology, "That wasn't really me." In a moment of failure, you can acknowledge you chose to live by your *old, corrupt self*. But Jesus has gifted you a new self who doesn't sin. That is the self who will exist in heaven for eternity. So you can focus on living according to that new self without guilt or shame or trying to atone for anything. Look again at Ephesians 4:

> *[You were taught] to put off your old self, which belongs to your former manner of life and is corrupt through deceitful desires, and to be renewed in the spirit of your minds, and to put on the new self, created after the likeness of God in true righteousness and holiness.*
>
> *(Ephesians 4:22-24)*

As a Christian, you can look at your dark side square in the eye and know—that it doesn't define you. You can confess this dark side of your self to Jesus and receive his forgiveness because of his death on the cross for that darkness. And with that repentance and faith in Jesus, you receive a new self—a Jesus-united self. Jesus renews you into that authentic version of your self. It's the best version of your self. It's who you were meant to be and would have been if sin had never come into the world in the first place. It's a vision of the mature you, complete with your perspective and giftings but magnified with love, humility, and self-control.

In its honest teaching about our sinful nature, then, the Bible gives you hope. It gives you a way to see, love, and be proud of an authentic version of your self, while hating and fighting against the other authentic, but sinful version of your self.

So how do you do that?

Reclaiming a Dirty Word

The Bible calls you to cultivate ("put on") your Jesus-self, and to repress and squash ("put off") the old, sinful self. I realize I just said the "r" word: repress. That's a dirty word right now, but it's one we've got to bring back if we want to thoroughly pursue our best authentic self. Today, if you tell someone to repress a desire, you might as well have told them to stab themselves in the groin. That's self-harm. What kind of sick and twisted advice is that? But this response is absurd. We do in fact tell people to repress desires all the time.

When seven-year-old Marcella keeps shouting out in class about her new puppy and the teacher tells her to stop, the teacher will not apologize and backtrack when Marcella responds, "But I *want* to!" Or think about how you spend your money. There are plenty of things this past week that you wanted to buy, but you repressed one or two of those desires. That didn't feel good, but you knew that it was the best choice for you in the long term.

Somewhere along the line, we've swallowed the absurd and unsustainable belief that at no point in time should we seek to change ourselves in a way that doesn't immediately *feel* good. Repressing anything (words, feelings, desires, or impulses) will never *feel* good, but that doesn't mean you shouldn't do it.

Take the classic novel *Dr. Jekyll and Mr. Hyde*, which is a masterpiece of identity conflict. It's about a doctor who invents a way to split himself into two selves so that he never has to repress his darker side. Dr. Jekyll is the civil, professional, socially acceptable self. Mr. Hyde is the grotesque self who lives out all his dark desires. As the story progresses, Hyde gets worse and worse, and Jekyll begins to lose control. It turns out the two selves can't peacefully coexist. One of them must kill the other.

That's how the Bible sees our identity struggle as well. "We know that our old self was crucified with [Jesus] in order that the body of sin might be brought to nothing ... So you also must consider yourselves dead to sin and alive to God in Christ Jesus" (Romans 6:6, 11). Your destructive, corrupt, sinful self was crucified when you believed in Jesus. It's as if Jesus took that self with him, and it was nailed to the cross. Its ownership over you as a Christian is dead.

But you still need to do the work of killing the influence of this old self. That won't feel good. It's like God pays for you to have your own custom fashion designer, but you still must resist the temptation to buy knock-off t-shirts from Amazon. Those tees just feel so familiar and convenient, and they're constantly being sold to you. How do you get the strength of will to resist them? One thing that will help you follow through on the daily death of self-denial is if you can see your old self for what it is—a grotesque disfigurement, like Mr. Hyde.

Again, Ephesians 4 is helpful. It urges you to put off your old self which is "corrupt through deceitful desires" (Ephesians 4:22). We've got to slow down to understand this. You will experience desires that are authentic *but deceitful.* They promise satisfaction and happiness, but that's a lie. At the same time, you will feel competing desires from God that call you upward. Your journey towards becoming who you are in Jesus is the high calling of listening to and following those God-given desires.

Faking It, Authentically

Early on in ministry, I sat down with an older pastor and confessed that I was feeling inadequate and incompetent. I worried about how that might be affecting people I was trying to help. Maybe they sensed my insecurity and were hesitant to trust me. This was his advice: "Fake it until you make it." I couldn't believe this was the actual counsel coming from a mature pastor. But slowly, I realized that's what I've been doing my whole life. That's what we all do.

Think about it: does a teacher teach before they're a teacher, or are they a teacher before they teach? It's one of those chicken-or-egg questions. Who you are shapes what you do, but then what you do shapes who you are. *All* of us are faking it until we make it—that's the only way to become something.

You will feel some disingenuousness as you attempt to live into your Jesus-self. It *doesn't* feel totally natural. How could it? And so you may start to wonder, "Am I being fake here?" But if we confine authenticity to only doing what feels familiar and natural, no authentic person would ever learn how to ride a bike, speak another language, or make a new dish.

There's some nuance here. Let's take an example: Shannon breaks up with her boyfriend, Kyle. Kyle has a female friend, Lucy, who takes to social media to blast Shannon's integrity and criticize the way she did the breaking up. Shannon feels angry. How should she respond? Given what I've just said about faking it, you might think that if she's living out her Jesus-self, she should pretend not to be angry—faking a calm and forgiving response while she boils inside. But that is not quite what it looks like.

Back in Ephesians 4, Paul uses anger as a practical example of how you put off the old self and put on the new self: "Be angry and do not sin" (v 26). There's a dividing line here between feelings over which you have little control (being angry), and actions which you do control (sinning). There's a pause—a deliberate step between feeling and doing. Paul doesn't tell us not to be angry—Shannon doesn't have to pretend that Lucy hasn't hurt her. But she *can* take the vital step of processing her anger in order to respond the right way—according to her new Jesus-self.

Mark 3:1-6 tells the story of a crowd that's gathered around Jesus, ready to accuse him if he heals a man with a "withered hand" on the Sabbath. It says that Jesus "looked around at them with anger." But it's important to note the reason why: because of "their hardness of heart" (v 5). After they reveal their self-righteous callousness, Jesus gets angry. That feeling is certainly not a sin—he's rightfully angry! But what does Jesus do with that anger? He turns away from the crowd. He doesn't engage with them, but simply does what is right and loving: he heals the man.

What could it look like for Shannon to be like Jesus? She'll start by considering why she's angry. Is she angry because Lucy is portraying her unfairly? That would be natural.

Is she angry because Lucy is right—Shannon didn't go about the breakup in the best way, and now that's been exposed? That would be less defensible. The point is that there is a moral sorting of emotions in search of what is underneath and what is the best way forward.

Let's say Shannon feels legitimate anger because she's been slandered. The next question is: how should she respond? In the quiet of her room, she hears two contending selves, each one demanding a different authentic response. One self is Shannon the strong and fierce woman. She is a force to be reckoned with and feared. She is not the sort of person to take that kind of cheap shot lying down. There will be consequences. Kyle and Lucy will rue the day that they crossed Shannon.

The other self is Shannon the strong and loving woman. She gets that from beholding and imitating Jesus. She's the sort of person who rises above because her security doesn't depend on what people think of her—she's a beloved child of God, and that's enough. This Shannon will take her anger to Jesus and a couple of trusted friends and then be capable of responding to Lucy with grace and equanimity. She lets the haters roll off her back, and what's more shocking, she'll even return them a kind word. She does not accept lies, but she's not shaken by them.

Both of those voices represent authentic selves. They're both *real* Shannons. But she will have to make a choice about which one to listen to. She will cultivate one authentic self and repress the other.

The Spirit-Fueled Self

Where does Shannon get the strength to do this? It's already there. God created this new self in her when she believed in Jesus. She has a new identity now, and this new self will win out as she beholds Christ. That's his promise (Philippians 1:6).

For Shannon and for us, cultivating our best self has to do with values. If you take a look at the fruit of the Spirit in Galatians 5:22-23, they're all values or character traits: "love, joy, peace, patience, kindness, goodness, faithfulness, gentleness, self-control." These are traits God is growing in your new Jesus-self. Your identities of origin, role, and affinity will shape your specifics in terms of how you express anger, hurt, forgiveness, and love. But we can know with certainty the *direction* our best authentic selves should go in.

The fruit of the Spirit comes naturally when we are beholding Jesus, as we talked about in chapter 2. As we center our master identity on Jesus and our relationship with him, we will be motivated by his love. We will see how he's patient and forgiving to us even when we deserve anger, and we will want to live into that authentic version of our self. Yes, sometimes it will feel like we're faking it—forcing ourselves into self-control, pretending to be cheerful—but as we keep "putting on" these actions and values, we'll find that they become who we truly and naturally are.

In one sense, a Christian putting on her new self and putting off her old self will look just the same as what Satir described—discarding what is unfitting. The clothing metaphor is even the same. But the Bible offers a beautiful objective clarity that Satir lacks. We can find a clear and unchanging vision of our new self in the character of Jesus—discerning which of our desires are good and which are bad by looking at him, the perfect human. And in Jesus, too, we find the power to put off the old self and put on the new.

As a Christian, you have a new Jesus-self. It's the best version of your self, brimming with love and goodness. You will spend the rest of your life growing into this authentic self. You will grow in learning which of your desires, words, and actions belong to that new, ideal self, versus the ones that come from your old, sinful self. That is how you can be authentic while becoming authentically better.

What do these selves look like for you? Where do you see an old self that keeps trying to kill you through deceitful desires that you need to repress? How can you picture these desires leading you to a grotesque self you don't want to become?

The question that is harder, but more important is: Where do you see your new Jesus-self? Where do you see flashes of best self—enjoying connection with God, others-focused, and content? What activities or friendships will help you cultivate that self?

Questions for Discussion and Reflection

1. Where have you seen examples of good authenticity? How is that different from bad authenticity?
2. How can the spiritual reality of a new Jesus-self living with an old, sinful self help you honestly confess when you've done wrong or need to change?
3. Review the last two paragraphs of this chapter and do your best to really answer the questions they pose.

CHAPTER 5

Living Free

The second way you become more like Jesus is to think of yourself as his servant. That doesn't sound great. Really, if we use biblical language, it's more accurate to think of yourself as his slave. That doesn't sound any better. How could being your best self involve living in a state of perpetual servitude? Therein lies the problem: you don't realize that you already are.

What Is Living Free?

What does it mean to live free? We understand freedom more by feeling than definition. Think about a sixteen-year-old boy studying chemistry during the last hour of school on a sunny afternoon. The bell rings. His palm hits the exit door. He breathes fresh air. He's free!

That feeling—that initial gust of exhilarating liberation—*that's* what we have in mind when we think about freedom. Why? Because we tend to view freedom negatively (as opposed to positively). It's always freedom *from*. The sixteen-year-old boy is free *from* the prison walls of the school, *from* a class he doesn't like, and *from* a teacher he didn't choose. He's free *from* the institution, the rigidity, the myriad of adults parading around in authority over him. Philosopher Isaiah Berlin called this negative freedom.[14]

But Berlin also talked about another type of freedom: the positive kind. Positive freedom is having the capacity to do the things you want to do, even though you may still experience restrictions. In other words, it prioritizes what your freedom is *for* rather than what it is *from*.

What do we want to be free *for*? "Worry about that when you get there!" our world says. "For now, make sure you're free *from* outside interference so that you can determine what you want for yourself." But as it turns out, becoming free *from* is not so easy. Our pursuit of freedom becomes its own lifelong slavery.

Over and Against the Power Brokers

The goal of identity construction in our culture is to achieve absolute negative freedom (freedom from everything). But the agents of oppression are always multiplying.

They (whoever they are) are always out to control you. "Don't let them get you," our world says. "Fight for your freedom." Behind every law, every advertisement, every election, every sudoku, there's a dark, smoky board room filled with old men in suits buying and selling you like properties in Monopoly. Society is nothing but large, ominous power agendas constantly pushing and pulling at you, trying to stamp out your individuality.

You may think you bought that pair of shorts because you liked them, but don't be naive. You are an unthinking pawn, you purchaser of shorts. You are putty, being manipulated by culture, corporate marketing, customs, traditions—in short, society, which serves the interests of the powerful. Freedom, therefore, is over and against these power brokers, who are everywhere. If you don't see them, it's because you're part of the senseless herd. If you're not fighting, it's because you're not free. Wake up!

There are useful truths you can discover in this suspicious mindset. Everyone *does* have an agenda. Everyone *is* self-interested. This is the case in the obvious spheres of business, politics, and religion but also in what were once our most cherished icons of objectivity. Fields that we want to believe are cordoned off by gatekeepers of data and due process—science, medicine, and academia—we find distressingly subject to politics, big business, and personal ambition.

It's good to be aware of this, but it's bad news when it comes to self-creating your identity. You're never going to get left alone in some corner to figure out who you are in undisturbed reflection. Instead, you go through life like a car wash—sprayed, soaped, wiped, buffed, and blasted from all directions from the power brokers who are trying to shape your identity for their own purposes. As you see this battle pressing against you from all sides, it's natural to wonder, "Can I ever be free? How will I know if I am?"

A Gladiator's Purgatory

Our world's answer is not pretty: you *can't* know. You're always being manipulated by someone. If you stop fighting, you've surrendered. The Empire has won.

Michel Foucault, a twentieth-century philosopher and pioneer of identity confusion, said that "freedom is not the abolition or destruction of power, but a relationship of permanent provocation."[15] In other words, you can't ever get away from power dynamics. You will spend your life as a gladiator in the arena, fighting off one group after another, who are all trying to control you. Foucault says that instead of using the word "freedom," we should speak of "agonism"[16]—a fitting word to describe this lifestyle. If you're not feeling some level of agony in your fight against The Man, it's because you took the blue pill and opted to live comfortably in the Matrix.

This pursuit of negative freedom means that your ideal identity is always becoming but never being. There's always a new target—a new enemy to your freedom. Trying to live free under those parameters will always feel exhausting and uncertain.

It's like the scene from the movie *The Princess Bride* where the hero, Westley, challenges the bandit leader Vizzini to a battle of wits. Westley tells Vizzini he has placed poison in one of their two cups, and challenges him to choose one cup; then they'll both drink. Vizzini reasons aloud over which cup he believes Westley has put the poison in, but he keeps realizing that Westley may have already counted on Vizzini reasoning that way and still be one step ahead. So Vizzini's reasoning keeps expanding: "But you know that I know that you know that I know that you know that I know... so you put the poison in *that* cup. But... you knew that I would think like that! So..." And on it goes. That is where freedom as infinite resistance leads us. Yet this is the road to freedom that our culture points toward, then says essentially, "Good luck!"

This endless pursuit of negative freedom means that you can't even trust any kind of universal guiding principle or moral code to help you figure out what to do or where to go. According to much of American culture, religion and tradition are twin evils that seek to squeeze and mold you, like all the rest. You have to reject them. Berlin says that the idea that moral principles could be universal is simply "a craving for the certainties of childhood or the absolute values of our primitive past."[17] In other words, if you feel certain about some set of absolute beliefs, that's only because you want to be a baby. So, what is the alternative? The life of never-ending fight.

The fight to live free becomes so all-consuming that it swallows up any consideration of what happens after you've *become* free. No one pauses to answer the question of "What will you do with your freedom once you get it?" Instead of freedom serving as the vehicle to move you towards your best authentic self, it becomes the end in itself. It's all about what you *shouldn't* conform to, and you're never left a moment to think about who you *should* be. But there's a better way.

How to Really Be Free

True freedom begins with recognizing that no one is absolutely free in the negative sense. So stop trying to be. Instead, seek positive freedom—that's the capacity to do things you want to do, even if you're still restricted. Realize that you will *always* have a master of some kind, so to become your best self, you need to find the best master. That's God. True freedom means acknowledging that one Master and taking on his empowering constraints. That's what Jesus meant when he said, "Take my yoke upon you ... For my yoke is easy, and my burden is light" (Matthew 11:29-30).

Freedom Is Finding the Right Restrictions

Tim Keller puts it this way:

> *Freedom is not, then, simply the absence of restrictions, but rather consists in finding the right, liberating restrictions. Put another way, we must actively take tactical freedom losses in order to receive strategic freedom gains.*[18]

Your pursuit of freedom is bound up in your vision of your best authentic self. Keller goes on to use the example of a concert pianist. How did she become that person? Every day, for several hours a day, she "gave up her freedom," to practice. She chained herself to that piano and did not permit herself to do anything else. She rigorously restricted herself. Why? In order to play powerfully, to move people's hearts and souls, and to enjoy a stunning freedom by way of newly opened doors, elevated experiences, and privileged opportunities for her to express herself. That is freedom.

Your freedom never works as raw and random self-will. It's always connected with your identity. You fight for freedom in order *to become* something. There is some good, some desire, some vision that your best authentic self wants to pursue, so you free yourself from interference for the sake of that goal.

To sum it up, we might define freedom like this:

Freedom is the capacity to be who you were made to be.

If we understand freedom this way, rules and restrictions make sense. God's purpose is that we flourish into our best selves. His constraints are not limitations on our freedom; they're given to us as a gift and a guideline to help us achieve freedom, like the piano player's disciplined practice. Freedom that is defined by and dependent on God "is not a restriction, but a specification, a way of characterizing its particular nature ... [Just as] life is no less life because it is given, so also freedom is no less freedom because it comes from God."[19]

Think about God himself. In what sense is he free? Well, he is *not* free to *not* be God. His character is unchanging—it is why he revealed himself to Moses as Yahweh, "I AM WHO I AM" (which also translates as "I WILL BE WHO I WILL BE", Exodus 3:13-14). God always acts according to his unchanging character—he moves only in certain ways. So, it is impossible for God to be unjust, to break his word, or to do wrong, because that's not who he is. His attributes are eternally constant, so in one sense he is not free, because he is not free to act against his character. This actually makes him more free, though, not less. God is free to be exactly who he is, in the full force of his goodness.

God will always be God. He is not checked by inconsistencies, doubt, or contradictions. God is straightforward—not an emotionally volatile child with his desires swinging all around, getting the best of him. You never have to worry about which version of God you will get. There is only one version of God, and he is always good.

No one is more free than God, and yet that "freedom" does not mean being free to go beyond or against his identity. The same principle is true for us. Freedom is a stream of water rushing through one focused channel instead of a pitcher poured out on a pavement. Here's the definition again: freedom is the capacity to be who you were made to be.

Everyone's a Slave

So who were you made to be? Whatever you believe to be the answer to that question, you will choose the things that get you closer to that answer. The trouble (as we saw in chapter 4) is that sin (both the devil and your sinful nature) presents us with confused pictures of who we should be and what we should want. So then, naturally we do confused and wrongheaded things while we pursue the wrong picture.

Sin whispers the lie that you're not really free if you follow God because you're restricted from doing the things that would take you off track. But it omits the truth that following a sinful track toward the wrong self also restricts you. It restricts you from doing things that would move you closer to God.

For example, sin will tell you, "Why tie yourself down sexually or emotionally to one person? You're giving up all these freedoms—all these possibilities!" That's a half-truth. If you reject the restrictions of monogamy, you're still enslaved. You're restricting yourself to a certain superficiality. You're restricting yourself from the depth, trust, comfort, and personal growth that come through exclusivity and commitment through decades of life together.

In other words, wherever we turn, we're going to be restricted. We're always choosing one option and closing off another. That's why the Bible calls *all* of it slavery. You're either a slave to sin, or you're a slave to righteousness.

> *Do you not know that if you present yourselves to anyone as obedient slaves, you are slaves of the one whom you obey, either of sin, which leads to death, or of obedience, which leads to righteousness? But thanks be to God, that you who were once slaves of sin have become obedient from the heart to the standard of teaching to which you were committed, and, having been set free from sin, have become slaves of righteousness. (Romans 6:16-18)*

Paul boils it down to two options. Everyone's ideal self belongs to one of two tribes: sin or righteousness. You *present yourself as an obedient slave* to that tribe because you're all in. You're sold on the picture of who you will become in that tribe. The real question, then, is not how can you be free, but which slavery will you choose? Which tribe do you want to be in?

When you become a Christian, it simply means that God's Spirit has gotten inside you and captured your imagination with the wonder of who Jesus is. You love the picture of the one who's representing this tribe of righteousness. You want to be with Jesus. You want to be *like* Jesus. You present yourself to him as an obedient slave, switching allegiance from your old tribal leaders of sin and death.

When you do this, you are offering every part of your life to Jesus to command. Your actions will change: "Do not merely listen to the word, and so deceive yourselves. Do what it says" (James 1:22, NIV). Your thinking will change: "Take every thought captive to obey Christ" (2 Corinthians 10:5). Your emotions and desires will change: "Where your treasure is, there your heart will be also" (Matthew 6:21). You offer your doing, thinking, and feeling to Jesus, for him to direct, because you want to be free his way. You want to be who you were made to be. You trust him to lead you into that.

Freedom from Others... Even Yourself!

As you pursue your freedom for the goal of becoming like Jesus, you'll find that you gain freedom from other things along the way. This begins in your head. You get a new way of evaluating yourself, free from anyone else's take. The apostle Paul writes, "With me it is a very small thing that I should be judged by you or by any human court. In fact, I do not even judge myself" (1 Corinthians 4:3). Now *that* is freedom! Can you imagine living your life free from second-guessing? You would still make mistakes and learn, but there would be only one objective, trustworthy, and loving judgment you would ever bother with—God's. And in Jesus, God's overall verdict is already in. He loves you, accepts you, and delights in you. You can be free from insecurity, uncertainty, and lack of confidence because your identity is already established.

The deepest freedom of all comes when you let go of ultimate responsibility. Without God, you are ultimately the one on the hook. You feel a burden of responsibility to others and yourself, yet you can never be certain about how well you're performing. Christian freedom, however, is a blissful "freedom from the care of self."[20] As a Christian, you know that even when you're getting it wrong, there is someone looking out for you who is getting it right. He can take even your worst failings and fold them into his plan to make you into your best self.

Freedom from care of your self is the reason why, for many, childhood feels so free and its memories glow with nostalgia. In the words of the band Twenty One Pilots: "I was told when I get older, all my fears would shrink / But now I'm insecure, and I care what people think."[21] At a superficial level, you are extremely *un*free as a child. You live in continual, overt dependence. You submit to a multitude of restrictions. But if you are blessed with responsible and loving parents, you have a free spirit that soars to heights that are unparalleled in adulthood. You are free from the need to care for yourself. Your parents hold that responsibility. That's what God wants you to regain if you recognize that he holds both you and the world in his hands.[22]

Jesus invites his followers to take his "yoke" upon them—referring to the restriction placed on oxen so that their owner can guide them while they work (Matthew 11:29-30). This sounds like a bad deal unless you realize that you are always under someone's yoke. Jesus' good news is that his "yoke is easy and [his] burden is light" (Matthew 11:30).

Listen to a verse that comes right before: "Come to me, all who labor and are heavy laden, and I will give you rest" (v 28). Jesus isn't talking to people who are roaming free, enjoying an unfettered life, because he knows that's none of us. No, he's talking of those who labor and are heavy laden. Jesus says something like, *Are you tired of pulling a cartload full of expectations? One that's crushing you to the ground? Are you tired of trying to pull different carts every day, each one feeling heavier than the last? Try mine. I'm going to lead you on the path to become who you're meant to be—the pathway of freedom.*

The Christian's Fight Is About Staying Free

Our world is partially right about freedom—it is a fight. As a Christian, though, you fight to stay free. "For freedom Christ has set us free; stand firm therefore, and do not submit again to a yoke of slavery" (Galatians 5:1). Sin is always trying to pull you down toward a distorted, disfigured version of your self. Don't let it. It will make the pathway toward that deformity look like freedom—but it's just the freedom to ruin yourself. The difference in following Jesus' path to freedom is that you can have confidence in the destination. You're becoming who you were made to be.

In contrast to the world's fight for freedom, a Christian's fight is not forever. Your sense of fighting actually diminishes over time as the obedience of freedom becomes easier. When you choose the freedom of serving Jesus, he promises "you will find rest for your souls" (Matthew 11:29). Life's not meant to be a never-ending struggle of uncertainty—fighting, fighting, fighting in every direction at all times till your dying breath. As you become more of your Jesus-self, the fight for freedom relaxes. You experience a stillness—a rest that comes over you when you are truly free.

One of the best illustrations of this is a freedom we've almost entirely lost in the past fifty years—the Sabbath. Not long ago, most of American society lived under many Sabbath restrictions. They were called blue laws. There wasn't much you could do in the way of shopping, dining out, and sports leagues on a Sunday. We've pivoted away from that now as too restrictive—too legalistic. But the point of those restrictions was freedom. You were free from many other occupations so that you could spend time in worship, reflection, rest, and enjoying family and friends. Are people really happier spending one more day running around working, buying stuff, and going to volleyball practice?

Recently, a number of young people have started practicing a digital sabbath—shutting down their phones for a day or at least a portion of it. What does that feel like? At first, it will feel like an inconvenient restriction. Maybe a little stupid. Why can't I just be free to use my phone when I want to use it? To maintain that restriction will feel like a fight—like self-denial. But on the other side of that restriction, you gain the ability to be more present in the moment. You experience a greater peace and freedom.

That's how "freedom for" becoming like Jesus works. Using your phone is not a sin, but the felt experience of pain in resisting its draw is similar to what you feel in resisting the temptation of sin. And—if you endure—you will find yourself free for meaningful and enriching times of reflection, conversation, and rest that you didn't have otherwise.

Your fight against sin never goes away completely, but it diminishes on the other side of experiencing the new freedoms you gain. You won't want to go back. As you compare your new freedoms with the ones you've lost, you'll find it is like exchanging a stroll outdoors for being served hospital food in a sickbed, and you'll wonder why you didn't want to get there faster. (See Romans 6:20-22.)

Questions for Discussion and Reflection

1. What's something you're fighting for more freedom *from* right now? What right restrictions might help you?
2. Where do you most often need to remember God's evaluations instead of the evaluations of others?
3. What does it look like in practice to fight to stay free?

CHAPTER 6

Telling a Story

The original Star Wars trilogy came out from the late 70s to early 80s, and it's still capturing imaginations today. It brings you into a world of underdogs, tyrants, mentors, mercenaries, and hostile environments. It pits good versus evil, sacrifice versus ambition. In short, it feels real. It feels like it could be your life: only the drama is cranked up and taking place in another galaxy in an alternative universe.

Star Wars has given hundreds of millions of people a story to make sense of their own story. Same with Harry Potter, The Lord of the Rings, and even the Marvel Cinematic Universe. That's what good stories do! They offer you an escape into another world, taking you on a journey where you emerge with strength and insight to face your own journey in your own world.

Take Aesop's famous fable "The Tortoise and the Hare," written in the 6th century BC. A hare and a tortoise race each other. The hare jumps way out ahead but then gets cocky and sleeps for several hours. Meanwhile, the slow and steady tortoise passes him by. The hare wakes up and sprints, trying to make up the distance, but the tortoise is too far ahead by now and wins the race.

We still refer to this story today to invoke the moral of "slow and steady wins the race." Few people, I imagine, believe this story is meant as a betting tip for future races that could take place between actual reptiles and long-eared mammals. Track coaches aren't using this as a strategy for their athletes. People do not take the moral of the story as an absolute, believing that "slow and steady" wins the race to the emergency room.

What you do take away from the story of "The Tortoise and the Hare" are categories and pictures that you can easily layer over your own life experience in a way that has rung true for over 2,500 years. Everyone can call to mind that brilliant and talented classmate who was running circles around everyone and who could have had his pick of careers. He was a gifted young man, destined to go places, but then he got complacent and napped away the race of his life. On the other side, you can see the remarkable fruit that comes from slow and dogged perseverance. Years of bland, monotonous reading, homework, and test-taking eventually bring you to the finish line of a degree and new opportunities. Micro-deposits and compound interest add up over time. The plodding piano player practicing scales one day reaches the finish line to become an accomplished performer.

The story of "The Tortoise and the Hare" gives you a complete picture that your mind can easily file away as a shortcut to understand what you're doing and why. We collect and file these stories almost unconsciously to help us make sense of what we're seeing in the world. Stories, not abstract ideas, are the framework on which we build our lives.

Identity Is Telling a Story

What does this have to do with becoming your best self? Identity construction is storytelling. You construct the story of your life. You revise, retell, add new chapters, develop characters, struggle through conflict, and find the morals you're supposed to be learning. Your identity journey is at the center of that story. Who are you and who are you becoming?

Social media uses the word "stories" to capture what we're doing when we curate words, pictures, and videos into one package. The process does as much for the storyteller as for anyone who sees the story. The same goes for when someone asks the question "How was your day?" You answer that by telling a story. In the act of telling the story, you are making sense of the day for yourself. What *was* important? How did you feel? Why did you feel that way? Why did the day develop the way it did? You are weaving together minutes and hours, activities and conversations, frustrations and encouragements into one single story to make sense of your life that day. Because of this, our lived experience is the act of imagining ourselves in a story. We're subconsciously recounting the day as we live it.[23]

We're constantly trying on different stories to see what fits. What rings true to my experience? What helps me explain where I've come from and where I am going? What story is the one I *want* to live into? If you're not happy with the conclusions it's leading to, you start over with a different script; you try on a different story.

Stories as Therapy

The most popular form of therapy today, cognitive-behavioral therapy (CBT), makes use of this psychological power of stories. The premise, as you can hear in the term itself, is that if you change your *thinking* (cognition) you will change your *acting* (your behavior). You act in accord with the story that you believe you are living. So therapy focuses on breaking down the story you're telling yourself and finding a better one.

It goes like this. You sit down with your therapist and recount an incident from last week that you're still stewing over: your friend Jerry mentioned that he helped his sister, Monica, move into her new house. Jerry knows you recently got your realtor's license. So, what gives? Why didn't he refer Monica to you? It's because Jerry's selfish, you reason. He's not a good friend. He and Monica probably enjoyed a good laugh over the idea of you trying to sell her house; then went and found someone competent.

Your therapist listens; then points out that you have constructed an entire story in your own head to explain this incident. This story is making you anxious and irritable, especially toward Jerry. But it's not the only story you can use. It's probably not the true story, and it's definitely not the best story for you as a realtor. You need to drop this current story and try on some different ones.

There are certain immovable facts in your original story that it's best you don't try to do away with. Monica is Jerry's sister; they're close enough that he helped her move. She did not ask you to be her realtor. But there are many possible storylines that interpret and connect these dots. You can ask Jerry, of course, but even then, you might not get the true story. Maybe Monica already knew someone. Maybe you don't have enough experience yet.

The therapist will likely tell you to focus on a larger story. What can you control? How does this incident fit in with your growth as a realtor? How do you move forward in the story of your friendship with Jerry? These are ways of reframing that small story by asking the questions that will place the incident into a better story. *I'm growing as a realtor. Rejection and failure come with trying anything new. I'm going to learn from this challenge and become stronger.* You're now telling yourself a better story.

In their article turned book *The Coddling of the American Mind*, Greg Lukianoff and Jonathan Haidt rest their hopes for Gen Z on this type of therapy. They point to an epidemic of mental fragility exacerbated by parents and eventually universities coddling rather than preparing young people.[24] The modern-day creation of "safe spaces," they argue, is a school's way of teaching that the solution to discomfort is to change the reality around us, not to change the story we're telling ourselves about it. This solution sets students up for cruel disillusionment and failure. Cognitive-behavioral therapy, Lukianoff and Haidt argue, is the panacea for today's mental health crisis.

CBT is nothing new. It is the modern West's rightful heir to a long strain of philosophy going back to Buddha, who said that "Life is the creation of our mind." A few hundred years after that, the Stoic philosopher and Roman emperor Marcus Aurelius said, "Life itself is but what you deem it."[25] Jonathan Haidt believes that CBT is carrying this torch. He says, "You can never achieve happiness by making the world conform to your desires, but you can master your desires and habits of thought."[26]

Buddhism, Stoicism, and cognitive-behavioral therapy have enjoyed such lasting success because they combine two powerful truths about identity formation: givenness and storytelling. They teach that you can live by the following two principles:

1. Most things in life are givens; you shouldn't try to control those things.
2. You do (and should) control your story *about* those givens.

These principles can be tremendously liberating, but you should have some hesitations. Shouldn't we want the *real* story, not just one that works for me right now? Surely it's better to tell a story of uncomfortable truth rather than comfortable self-delusion.

In some ways, however, a Christian looking to become his or her best self will be nodding along with these common-grace principles. *Yes, yes, life is full of givens, and you need to tell yourself the true story about these givens to navigate them well.* But what should that story be? That's the question. Where is the story of your life going? Is there a stable and specific answer to that?

Your identity is your sense of self that connects who you are as a product of your past with who you wish to be in the future. How do you tell that story in a way that is true?

Jesus' Story Is Your Story

The good news is that the Bible has an answer. And it's a story that doesn't ask you to shut down and feel less, like Stoicism. As a Christian, you have one true story to tell with your life. It's Jesus' story being played out in you. You are becoming who you are by being transformed to look more and more like Jesus (2 Corinthians 3:18). But in this story, Jesus is the hero, not you.

What is this story? You lose the world to gain eternity (Matthew 16:25-26). You bear your cross as you wait for the crown.[27] You go down to go up (Luke 14:10). You humble yourself so God can exalt you (James 4:10). You give up your life to find it again (Matthew 10:39). In broad strokes, the story is death into resurrection.

Philippians 2:5-11 is a CliffsNotes version of Jesus' death-into-resurrection story. He humbled himself "by becoming obedient to the point of death, even death on a cross. Therefore, God has highly exalted him and bestowed on him the name that is above every name" (v 8-9). God himself set aside his rights and privileges, dying in the place of sinners, who wanted nothing to do with him. When you become a Christian, you receive this identity at the core of your being. So it is only natural that your life will track along the same storyline.

The initial act of becoming a Christian is the ultimate admission that you are not enough. You don't have what it takes. You can't get it together, and you need help in the worst possible way. But when you take that step, you receive the most exalted identity anyone could have—you become God's child.

The process of growing into and becoming your best self is a series of miniature deaths and glorious resurrections. You die to your own plans, your own will, your own desires. On the other side of those mini deaths, God gives you a resurrected self that is higher and more glorious than it was before. "We all, with unveiled face, beholding the glory of the Lord, are being transformed into the same image from one degree of glory to another" (2 Corinthians 3:18).

Redeeming, Not Rejecting

This process of dying feels scary because, well... dying is scary. It requires completely letting go of a thing with a willingness to never get it back again. But God's plan is never only death; it's also resurrection. He doesn't reject who you are. He redeems it and repurposes it. For example, when Jesus resurrected Lazarus in John 11, Lazarus didn't come out of the tomb as somebody else. Everyone could recognize him as the same old Lazarus but with a new lease on life.

Let's say one of your identities of origin was coming from a wealthy family. Taken the wrong way, that story can become a source of either pride or shame. Jesus' story is different. Jesus calls you to die to wealth's defining imprint on your life (Matthew 19:21-24). But that identity of origin isn't wrong. There's a resurrection story Jesus has for you. He wants you to delight in generosity (Luke 19:1-10) and to be strategic in how you use your privileged position for his kingdom (Luke 16:1-13).

How Paul Learned to Retell His Story

You won't find a more dramatic story of identity transformation than that of Saul becoming the apostle Paul. Saul, anti-church terrorist, became Paul, church planter and Scripture writer. God turns Paul's life on its head when he meets and saves him on the road to Damascus, as he's heading to lock up Christians (Acts 9). Yet afterward, there are many things about Paul that remain exactly the same.

Before conversion, Paul is a well-educated, driven, entrepreneurial leader. After conversion, Paul still is a well-educated, driven, entrepreneurial leader. He simply beholds a new destination—Jesus. What should encourage us is not only how much Paul changes, but how much he also stays the same.

God redeemed the raw identity material of the person of Paul by redirecting his focus. In Philippians 3, Paul shares how he has learned to retell his story with Jesus at the center. From a young age, Paul centered his identity on becoming a respected religious leader among the Jews. He lists off a long résumé of achievements that established his master identity of Jewish superstar:

> *Circumcised on the eighth day, of the people of Israel, of the tribe of Benjamin, a Hebrew of Hebrews; as to the law, a Pharisee; as to zeal, a persecutor of the church; as to righteousness under the law, blameless.*
>
> *(Philippians 3:5-7)*

He was born into the right kind of family. He studied under the best teacher (Acts 22:3). He learned the Scriptures by heart and threw himself into every rule and regulation the most zealous Jews were adhering to. Paul checked off all the identity boxes to be a superstar Pharisee. He outstripped all his peers in his pursuit of this master identity (Galatians 1:14).

This is how all of us tell our identity stories. As we look back over our lives and ahead into the future, we're trying to assemble a résumé that builds towards the position that we aspire to. We select material that tells the right narrative and discard the rest.

Jesus: Your Author, Hero, and Ending

Paul's encounter with Jesus changed the way Paul told his story:

> *But whatever gain I had, I counted as loss for the sake of Christ. Indeed, I count everything as loss because of the surpassing worth of knowing Christ Jesus my Lord. For his sake I have suffered the loss of all things and count them as rubbish, in order that I may gain Christ and be found in him. (Philippians 3:7-9)*

You can't change the ending of a story without reinterpreting everything that comes before. Star Wars would feel quite different if Jabba the Hutt ended up taking over the Empire. When Saul becomes Paul, the ideal ending of his story changes from him becoming a Jewish Pharisee superstar to knowing Christ Jesus. The hero of his story also changes—from Saul to Jesus. When Paul tosses everything about his past aside, he's not saying that he is rubbish; it's the story he was telling that was rubbish. He now has a new story.

> *... that I may know him and the power of his resurrection, and may share his sufferings, becoming like him in his death, that by any means possible I may attain the resurrection from the dead. (v 10-11)*

Paul begins retelling his own story as one of death and resurrection. He sees Jesus as the author, redeeming every one of his identities of origin, role, and affinity. Paul retains his Jewish culture and his love for the Jewish people, his identity of origin (Romans 9:2-3). He continues in his roles as teacher and leader (Acts 14:21-23). He still has an affinity for the frontlines of religious controversy (Galatians 2:11-14). But the only thing that now counts for his past or future is the story of his Jesus-self.

This new master identity recreates Paul's sense of self—the way he connects who he is as a product of his past with who he wishes to be in the future. There's a new, stable thread running through all his story—it's about knowing, sharing with, and being united to Jesus. His identity has become entirely about pursuing this relationship. And while he's living, it's not over: "Not that I have already obtained this or am already perfect, but I press on to make it my own, because Christ Jesus has made me his own" (Philippians 3:12). Even though Paul knows what his identity is about, his journey is not over. He's straining and pressing on to become who he already is.

Retelling Your Story

As Christians, God points us to one shared story: his redeeming work in Jesus. This is the story you should tell constantly—to yourself and others. When ancient Israel is about to enter the promised land, God tells them to immerse themselves and their children in his promises and commands, which flow out of their story of redemption from Egypt. He demonstrates that identity formation happens through telling stories that create values and commitments. "These words that I command you today shall be on your heart. You shall teach them diligently to your children, and shall talk of them when you sit in your house, and when you walk by the way, and when you lie down, and when you rise" (Deuteronomy 6:6-7). God's commands to Israel at that time included the whole Torah (the first five books of our Bible). It was not the full story we have today as Christians, but it was nevertheless the story of God as their Creator and Redeemer, and a call for God's people to respond in wholehearted obedience and faith. That is always the storyline of God's people.

We have the same need to repeat and internalize these stories. The story of the Exodus, of Israel's wandering in the wilderness, of their longing for a king, of the glory and inadequacy of David, of Israel's rebellion and exile—these aren't just stories with morals. They're *your* story, today. God is teaching you the same lessons, growing you in the same ways, giving you the same hope in his promise of salvation. The specifics are different—most notably we have a clear fulfillment of prophet, priest, and king in Jesus—but you will find the same principles of how God's people hope and endure through faith. As you retell your story with Jesus at the center, you can find wisdom and a deeper understanding of God's character by noticing Bible stories and themes that map over your experience.

Let's hover over the story of the Exodus. There's a way in which the whole Christian life is a wandering in the wilderness between your exodus (from the slavery of sin) and your arrival in the promised land (heaven). But there are microcosms of this story that also apply. Maybe you feel that God is opening a door for you to a new and better opportunity—a new job or a new location. It's an exodus. But once you get away from your past situation, your new one feels... not much better. It's not the promised land. It's a wilderness. You're questioning whether you ever should have left. You're questioning whether God knows what he's doing.

You need the principles found in the story of Israel's wilderness wandering to see what God is doing right now (Numbers 11 – 25). He's refining you (Numbers 16:25-26). He's getting you ready for the true promised land. Along the way, he's providing miraculous relief and deliverance (Exodus 17:1-7; Numbers 21:4-9).

Take another story—the story of David's greatness followed by his failure. It's there to help you process your own story when you fail or when seemingly godly and gifted leaders disappoint you. Even the best of people fail. Those failures and sins have ugly consequences (2 Samuel 12:10-11, 14). Everyone—except Jesus—will let you down. But that's not the whole story. God forgives. He restores (v 13). God brought redemption through Solomon, who led Israel to the height of their greatness, out of a marriage David began in dreadful sin. God is able to redeem and bring hope even when you fail. You need the wisdom of that story.

The Bible provides us with stories we can use to categorize our own experiences and bring them to God. Like any good story, the more you study the Bible's details, the more it will come alive to your experience today. The book of Psalms complements these stories by giving voice to the full range of our emotional experience. The way you find emotional satisfaction is not through stoic stiffening—learning to flatline your feelings. Nor is it in stuffing yourself with cotton candy mantras of positive thinking. It comes in bringing your emotions into the context of your relationship with Jesus, and receiving direction from his word in the Bible.

Let's go back to the story of you, the hypothetical realtor, with your friend Jerry and his sister Monica. Monica just bought a new house without asking for your help. How do you begin retelling this story? Start with the ending. What's this story really about? What is God's goal for you? How do you grow towards your best self in this story? It's by knowing, sharing with, and being united to Jesus more. You can know Jesus more in this story as someone who was rejected by his friends and doubted by his peers. You share in his sacrifice for those who were slighting and ignoring him, which includes you and me. And you're united with him in his resurrection in power.

You can trust in God to bring new good and growth out of your pain and loss.

You can share, even enjoy, a new layer of closeness in your relationship with Jesus in this small humiliation of being overlooked. You too can keep doing good. You too can keep serving and dying to your pride for the sake of Jerry and Monica. And you can know that in that process, God is resurrecting you into a more generous, forgiving, and glorious version of yourself—one that looks more like Jesus. One where the light of Christ in you shines brighter every day. That's your story.

Questions for Discussion and Reflection

1. What's your favorite book or movie? Why? What part of that story resonates with you?
2. Think of a key story from your life. How can Jesus' story of death and resurrection help you interpret what happened? How would it help you respond if you experienced the same thing today?
3. What Bible story, passage, or verse is relevant to your situation today? How can that give you hope in how Jesus is forming your identity?

CHAPTER 7

Relating to God

The novel *The Great Gatsby* tells a great tragedy. It's the story of how one relationship transforms a person's identity. Jay Gatsby achieves the rags-to-riches American dream. He reinvents himself completely—down to his very name—to become everything he imagines he is supposed to be for the girl he loves. Everything he does along his identity journey—the high-society manners he learns, the depths he descends into to make his illicit fortune, the place he chooses to live in, the house that he buys, the parties that he throws—all centers on pleasing one person.

Gatsby's obsession is Daisy Buchanan, a married woman that he previously loved and lost because he was too poor and low-class. Everything about the identity he forges is meant to recapture this lost relationship. Spoiler alert: he fails. But his story shows this principle: your most important relationship shapes your identity.

As humans born in sin, we've lost our defining relationship with God. More than anything else, we need to find our way back. It's only in this relationship that we can be ourselves and become who we're meant to be. But too often we're like a proud ex-boyfriend who would rather live miserable and alone than swallow his pride and admit he messed things up.

Fortunately, God knows we're never going to figure it out on our own. Jesus lived and died to mend this relationship. When we believe that, we re-enter this relationship with God. And all relationships, but especially your primary one, reshape your identity.

Identity Is Relationship

Listen closely the next time you hear someone sharing her life story. She's trying to explain her identity, especially her sense of self as a product of her past. But as she recounts her identities of origin, role, and affinity, what you will actually hear are words about her relationships.

Any identity of origin, role, or affinity loses meaning if you take out *the people* associated with that identity. For example, your place of birth (your origin) holds significance for your identity because of the culture (shaped by the people) of that place. Your role as a student has meaning because of your relationships with teachers and other students. Your affinity for Arsenal Football Club has meaning for your identity because of how you relate to the people on that team and, more importantly, to other fans.

God works this way too. When God meets Moses on Mount Sinai, he makes himself known. How does he do it? He describes his identity relationally:

> *The LORD, the LORD, a God merciful and gracious, slow to anger, and abounding in steadfast love and faithfulness, keeping steadfast love for thousands, forgiving iniquity and transgression and sin, but who will by no means clear the guilty. (Exodus 34:6-7)*

God reveals his identity in how he relates to people. The Lord is merciful and gracious *to people*. He is slow to anger that *people* provoke. He abounds in steadfast love *for those people* (who repent). God justly pardons sinners but also holds sinners accountable. God is just because of how he relates to *people*, not the Indian Ocean or the planet Jupiter. Because God is a person, he relates in a personal way to everything in the world. I'm not saying that God would become something less if there were no people—as if he would lose something. God existed for eternity before he created people and is complete in the Trinity. Yet God personally relates to every human being. No one can be relationally neutral with God, as if he were some force of gravity or karma.

To help us understand the nature of our relationship with him, God has given us three relational categories in the Bible that we can use as analogies: Creator-creature, father-child, and husband-wife. Let's examine each of these.

Creator-Creature Relationship

If you think of yourself as a creature and God as your Creator, that relational dynamic comes with great possibilities as well as hard boundaries. Your ceiling is high because as you become your best self, you're showing off your Creator through the gifts he created you with. This relational dynamic also establishes humility about your design, limitations, and relationship with other creatures, because you didn't make yourself. You are the property of your Creator.

A CREATURE SHOWS OFF THE CREATOR

"What is man that you are mindful of him, and the son of man that you care for him? You have made him a little lower than the heavenly beings and crowned him with glory and honor" (Psalm 8:4-5). Human beings are the crown of God's creation, which means we can aspire to show off God in a way that a cornfield never can. Our high position among created things comes with the high responsibility of more fully representing God. Your ability to think about and improve your identity bears witness to that. An iguana is not worried about becoming a better iguana. It reaches the best version of itself by sitting on a limb, chewing a leaf.

In Genesis 1:26, God makes it clear how great a creation we are compared to all the rest of it: "Let them [human beings] have dominion over the fish of the sea and over the birds of the heavens and over the livestock and over all the earth and over every creeping thing that creeps on the earth." Dominion is part of the two-sided coin of privilege and responsibility that reflects God—his position and responsibility of caring for the universe.

A CREATURE IS HUMBLE BEFORE THE CREATOR

Given our exalted position relative to the rest of creation, it's easy to get carried away. We need to remember our lowliness as well. We didn't make ourselves. God designed human beings and a fine-tuned world that we could live in. Remembering this truth creates a certain humility and restraint when it comes to shaping our identity. Take away the "I'm a creature" humility, and bad things happen. Your willingness, for example, to step on another person directly correlates with how far you've drifted from seeing yourself as merely one creature among many—who are all created in the image of God.

"Woe to him who strives with him who formed him, a pot among earthen pots! Does the clay say to him who forms it, 'What are you making?' or 'Your work has no handles'?" (Isaiah 45:9). Can you imagine a piece of putty in a ceramics class piping up, "Now hold on a second; I don't want to be another hourglass vase—so cliché! Have you considered making me a ribboned candy dish?" It's equally absurd for us to shoot back at God, "Really, God? Math skills?" Or "You left an inch off the top, God. Good try, but B+ effort on the whole."

This goes back to the issue of givenness. One of our most important tasks as creatures is to understand which givens are God's good design and which are really flaws. If we identify that some aspect of ourselves that we've been perceiving as an inescapable given is actually a way that sin has marred God's good design, we can seek God's help to overcome it.

For each of these relational dynamics, I'll give a one-word summary for how this type of relationship should move us to act. Here's the summary of your response to the Creator-creature relational paradigm: *reflect*. You, the creature, are a reflection of your Creator, no matter what. That will never change. There is something intrinsically good and beautiful about you because you reflect the image of God. You become better as you live into God's created design. You work with God's Spirit, who renews, polishes, and refines that image so that you reflect your Creator better.

You will always be a very specific sort of creation—a human being. A man or a woman. You will never be very happy if you spend your life wishing that you were a pine tree. And you will never make a particularly good pine tree. That's essentially what we're doing when we fritter away hours haunted by the wish that God had created us differently—perhaps as someone smarter, funnier, or prettier than we are. What you can do is reflect your Creator by becoming the best version of your self—a creature who is made in his image.

QUESTIONS FOR REFLECTION

- How might seeing yourself as God's creature made in his image give you both a higher and a humbler view of yourself?
- Where do you think you could be more receptive to God's instructions as your Creator?
- What's one way you would like to reflect God's glory to others more?

Father-Child Relationship

In one of Jesus' most famous parables, the Prodigal Son, Jesus attempts to correct the wrong impression we have of our father-child relationship with God (Luke 15:11-32). In the parable, there's a father with two sons. The sons go in opposite directions but both make the same mistake in how they think about their relationship with their father.

The younger son goes off the deep end. He took his inheritance and "squandered [it] in reckless living" (Luke 15:13). Why? We can guess that the answer is the same as why someone would run from God today. Maybe he feels that living with and working for his dad is a raw deal. All work and no play. His dad is boring, stuffy, and restrictive. He thinks his dad is a selfish taskmaster, an unfeeling maker of rules and lists. When he looks at his father, he doesn't see the real picture—of someone who loves him, knows what's best for him, and wants him to thrive.

The older son sees his father in the same distorted way, though his response is different. He figures, *I'll learn the lists and follow the rules. That way I'll earn a good life. I'll work for the good benefits and perks that I can earn from the boss* (Luke 15:29). Both sons fail to see their father as loving and sacrificial.

If we do not see God as a loving Father, then we become suspicious of his intentions and respond in one of these two self-destructive ways. We either run off into wild and reckless living, or we try to follow the rules and become bitter and self-pitying when we don't reap the benefits. Maybe we alternate between those two. But in the parable, the father reaches out to both sons with grace and forgiveness.

LIVING AS GOD'S CHILD

The Bible is full of instruction, direct and indirect, for how to live well. But how you respond to this instruction depends entirely on your relational identity with God. In an earlier chapter, we talked about how we are all slaves to something. But that's only one side of our relational identity. In Jesus, God elevates us from forced labor to part of the family.

How do you see yourself in relation to God? Are you merely a slave, or are you his child? "Slaves take liberty *from* duty; children have liberty *in* duty."[28] When you see yourself as a slave, your only opportunities for freedom come when you clock out or can avoid the watchful eye of your boss. As a child of a loving father, you find your freedom in your privileged responsibility to contribute to the family business.

If you see God as your loving Father, you have a better way to process everything that happens to you—the good and the bad. Living as God's child is not an identity restriction.

Rather, it opens the world up to you. You are God's heir (Romans 8:17). He disciplines you for your good, precisely because he's not apathetic. He loves you and cares deeply about how you turn out (Hebrews 12:7-11). He's not holding anything back from you. Instead, he wants you to enjoy everything he made to the max: "All things are yours, whether Paul or Apollos or Cephas or the world or life or death or the present or the future—all are yours, and you are Christ's, and Christ is God's" (1 Corinthians 3:21-22).

As we try to figure out our identity in relation to other people, our mortality, and our sense of self (a product of the past and who we wish to be in the future), God wants us to start with our relationship to him. If you've put your faith in Jesus, he's made you his child. If you're his child, then you belong to him. The whole world also belongs to him. And as his child, he offers you the world as a gift. You don't have to clutch for as much of it as you can close your fist around. It's all there for you. God is not trying to deprive you; he's like a dad showing you how to use the kite he gave you. It's not a basketball or a gardening tool; it's for flying. He wants to guide you.

A DAD YOU WANT TO IMITATE

All of us, to varying degrees, need to reset the broken paradigm of our father-child relationship because no father is perfect. But God is. He shows us what we want and need from a perfect father. The most prominent way that seeing God as a loving father seeps into your identity is through imitation. This is why God says things like "Be holy, for I am holy." (See Exodus 19:6; Leviticus 19:2; 1 Peter 1:16). What are you doing when you try to follow God's commands? You're not just checking off tasks on a set of daily directions dropped from heaven. You're imitating. The reason why God gives you commands and instructions is so that you can be like him, which is always for your good.

Jesus says, "Love your enemies and pray for those who persecute you" (Matthew 5:44). Why? Because "Just do it"? Because "Love wins"? No, it's "so that you may be sons of your Father who is in heaven. For he makes his sun rise on the evil and on the good, and sends rain on the just and the unjust" (Matthew 5:45). Every day God shows us how he loves his enemies. Jesus was imitating his Father as he died for his enemies. And he's designed us to mature by imitation. You grow into your best self by watching, learning about, and modeling your Father.

Maybe you've heard a mom say to her kid, "That's not how we talk in this house." Maybe you've used that line yourself. At face value, that's absurd. Clearly that is how we talk in this house because someone just did. But the mom means something completely different. She is leaning on relational identity formation. The mom and her kid are a "we." The security of the child's relationship is never in question. Rather, the mom invites and commands her child to become more like her. It's another way of the mom saying, "You are my child. Now become who you are."

Here's a one-word summary of your response to this relational paradigm: *imitate*. There is stability in your identity as a child. You will never be anything else. You will always be dependent on your Father. But you will also become more like him as you imitate him.

How will you live if imitating God your Father is a pillar of your identity? The only way to imitate someone is to spend time with them. Get to know God. Pray to him. Get into his mind and heart, which he's revealed in the Bible. Most of all, treasure that relationship.

QUESTIONS FOR REFLECTION

- What good traits of your father (or one you know) would you like to see better in God? What negative traits of your father are impacting your relationship with God? How can you work with God to rewire that thinking?
- How can knowing God as your powerful and loving Father give you more peace in unmet desires?
- What's one way you would like to imitate your heavenly Father?

Husband-Wife Relationship

I should say out of the gate that this one feels a little weird—but the Bible insists on using it, so it's important. Paul says that the mystery of marriage is profound because it refers to Christ (as the husband) and the church (as the wife) (Ephesians 5:32). John the Baptist calls himself a friend of the bridegroom, Jesus (John 3:29), and Jesus also refers to himself as the bridegroom (Matthew 9:15).

As a guy, I particularly don't gravitate toward thinking about Jesus as our husband. Either way, once you add in the sexual component of marriage, we're probably all profoundly uncomfortable. The weird factor is a good starting place because it's not as if God is thrown by this. He's not like your dad, accidentally using some old-fashioned phrase that has taken on sexual connotations. God is fully aware of the strangeness and intensity of this analogy, but he uses it anyway.

If we get squeamish thinking about God as our husband and ourselves as his wife, it's because we've got hold of the wrong end of the analogy. It's not as if God looked around, saw a loving marriage, and figured, "That's a good way to describe my relationship with my people." God created us for the express purpose of a relationship with him—one that would be unlike any other in this world. Then he created marriage to give us a picture of our relationship with him.

Our husband-wife relational design with God is the reason why we have happily-ever-after fairy tales. Take Cinderella. What's the enduring appeal of this story? You have a poor down-and-out gal hoping to be discovered by the prince. If she can finally be with this one right guy—the guy she's made for and who's in love with her—everything will be all right. They'll live happily ever after.

And that's how the story ends. That's only possible, however, if the prince is Jesus. Humanly speaking, Cinderella's marriage would be a real challenge. Happily-ever-after would involve sorting through class and cultural barriers, meeting in laws, and negotiating where the prince is going to store his hunting gear. But the fairytale ending points us to what we're made for in marriage with Jesus. There *is* strain and conflict in this marriage with Jesus, but all the selfishness is on one side. Ultimately, it really is happily-ever-after because we married perfection.

A great marriage is a lot of things—a friendship, partnership, a shared vision, and shared surrender. Through it all, there's a one-word summary of our response to this relational paradigm: *love*. We should love God like a wife loves her husband.

I want to look at a couple of attributes of a loving marriage that reflect the relationship God wants us to have with him: romance and mutual flourishing.

ROMANCE

Let's start with the weirdest one—at least when it comes to thinking about God. Can we really talk about being romantically involved with God? Truth is, our unwillingness to make connections between romance and God is the cause of some our deepest disappointments. No human relationship can sustain the desire we have to be swept up in a passionate romance. The intensity and excitement you want to feel when you think about a person you're in love with is a God-given desire that can point us toward what we're made for spiritually.

On the other hand, we often slide into a transactional paradigm in our relationship with God because that's mostly what we know. *I'll do a few things for God, then I'll have some favors in the bank.* If you approach any romance in that way, you're shortchanging yourself. That's not how God designed romance.

Romance involves a focus on and delight in the other person. In its best form, it includes a sense of mutual devotion and ownership that creates unwavering fidelity. That's what we discover with Jesus: "My beloved is mine, and I am his" (Song of Solomon 2:16). There's also a sweetness and enjoyment Jesus wants us to have with him.[29] "As the bridegroom rejoices over the bride, so shall your God rejoice over you" (Isaiah 62:5). "He brought me to the banqueting house [literally, his house of wine] ... I am sick with love" (Song of Solomon 2:4, 5). To be sick with love feels unsustainable. You can't get work done.

You can hardly hold a conversation. You just can't stop thinking about that other person. God doesn't intend for you to live in a constant state of lovesick intoxication, but that is a part of your relationship with him as a Christian. He delights in you down to every detail and wants you to do the same with him (Song of Solomon 4:1; Psalm 145:5-7).

MUTUAL FLOURISHING

Husband-wife relationships hold first-place identity significance because of the goal of that relationship combined with its intimacy. You're not teammates or coworkers. The goal isn't somewhere out there in a finished product or task. The goal is the other person. And unlike with children, there's no move-out date anticipated. Marriage brings you closer than anything else to joining in God's work of "helping each other become our future glory-selves."[30]

We need to see God as our husband because that's the clearest way we can be and become. You can simply *be* with God. In Jesus, you are loved, accepted, and cherished by God exactly as you are. You can't do anything to *become* more of God's bride. But you can become more of your best self—the person God designed you to become.

For our part, we don't cause God to flourish, but as we flourish together, we show more fully who God is and how great this relationship is. Tim Keller said that Christian marriage is "to look at another person and get a glimpse of the person God is creating, and to say, 'I see who God is making you, and it excites me! I want to be a part of that.'"[31] One spouse flourishing reflects well on the other. Husbands are to love their wives "as Christ loved the church and gave himself up for her, that he might sanctify her ... so that he might present the church to himself in splendor, without spot or wrinkle or any such thing, that she might be holy and without blemish" (Ephesians 5:25-27). As our husband, Jesus is part of not just declaring us holy but also making us more like him.

If we see God as our husband and his goal as our flourishing, it will bolster us through life's fires. As you go through the fire, you might not understand the process, but you know the goal and you know the one who's taking you toward it. You can know in the midst of uncertainty and disappointment and even plain boredom that Jesus is taking you toward what he wants his people to look like in heaven—splendid, without spot, wrinkle or blemish. You might wish that he ignored some of your spots, wrinkles, and blemishes, but you know he's relentlessly after your best because he loves you.

QUESTIONS FOR REFLECTION

- Why do you think God risks the misinterpretation/weirdness that comes with his analogy of a husband-wife relationship with us?
- Think about a command or life experience you find challenging. How could you see that as God's plan for your flourishing?
- What's one thing you can do to grow more in love with God?

Relating to God Is Complex but Rewarding

It's not possible to bottle your relationship with God into one single analogy. He is, after all, infinite. He is your Creator, Father, and husband. Each one of these relational categories has its own complexities. In that sense, building your identity on your relationship with God will not make your identity simpler. But it will give you the right kind of stability and growth, of being and becoming.

God himself is stable. He never changes, which means that the nature of your relationship with God never changes. God's never going to say, *Why don't you try being my father for a little bit?* Or *I think I'm done being your Creator.* When part of your relational identity is guaranteed like that, you don't have to worry whether you're wasting your time developing it.

These relational categories also give you trajectories for growth—for becoming. That's what we want with any part of our identity. Just because I am a husband doesn't mean I'm a good one. I want to grow into that identity. We spend all our lives running around, trying to grow into the identities that we believe are most important. (What does it look like for me to be an awesome mom, friend, entrepreneur, microbrewer, whatever?) The key is to keep refocusing on the right master identity—your relationship with God.

Questions for Discussion and Reflection

Review the reflection questions on pages 98, 102 and 106.

CHAPTER 8

Finding Community

In 2018, the UK government created a Minister for Loneliness. The problem has not improved. But the solution is simple: relationships, investing in others, and community. So, what's the hold-up? The reason those solutions *aren't* simple is because they require trespassing on one of the few temples we still venerate in the West—the autonomy of the individual. Underneath our culture's thoughts on authenticity, freedom, and identity, there is one unassailable premise: only you get to make your self.

Academy and Emmy award-winner Shirley McClaine put it this way back in the 70s:

> *The most pleasurable journey you take is through yourself ... The only sustaining love involvement is with yourself ... When you look back on your life and try to figure out where you've been and where you are going, when you look at your work, your love affairs, your marriages, your children, your pain, your happiness—when you examine all that closely, what you really find out is that the only person you really go to bed with is yourself. The only person you really dress is yourself.*

> *The only thing you have is working to the consummation of your own identity.*[32]

In other words, any time spent with others or for others is time wasted. It's getting in the way of the one and only thing you get to keep—your self-created self. Because of the pervasiveness of this belief in our culture, we can end up having a visceral fear of relationships and commitment. These things represent tying yourself to someone else's vision of who you should be. James, a 20-year-old, put it this way: "It's difficult to try to learn about yourself when you're with someone else."[33] Journalist Leigh Taveroff advises, "Your 20s are years where YOU DO YOU. Be selfish, have fun, and explore the world."[34]

This worldview creates some big problems. The most obvious one is poking us in the eye right now: loneliness. How can you enjoy deep and meaningful relationships if you've got to get rid of everyone else to figure out your self?

Since ancient times, young people have often done some rite of passage where they go off by themselves. You discover yourself in a new way when left *to yourself*. The difference, historically, was that young men and women returned to the community. Now life is one long string of these rites of passage—removing yourself from one community after another, always hoping to find a deeper knowledge of you.[35]

Another problem with siloed self-discovery is that it's simply not possible over the long haul. Our culture has set up a trap. You either feel inauthentic—that you're being shaped by someone else—or you end up lonely and still uncertain because you won't trust anyone else to test your conclusions.

The truth is that you can't discover who you are without other people. It's absurd to believe that you should excavate your true self by clearing the rubble of outside interference. You will never find such a thing. Your true self is always connected to other people. In the absence of real, known-and-knowing community, people wander into thin, transient digital communities that are cultivated by brands and celebrities.

The religion of secular consumerism supposedly offers a buffet from which you piece together your "self-constructed identity." You borrow from a celebrity here, an influencer there. You decide, for example, that you're the sort of person who can't stand the new Taylor Swift album, who drinks Coke, not Pepsi, and who attaches circle-stickers of your local coffee shop to the back of your MacBook. Or maybe you're just the opposite. Maybe you love Lululemon, Starbucks, your BMW, and anything that shouts mainstream affluence. The point is that you can't create an identity from the ground up. You create it in dialogue with a community. But does anyone in this community really know you or care about you personally?

This is a big reason why LGBT+ communities have had such success. They seem to deliver a thicker, more personal community—one that aims to bind together a wide range of personal expressions under a single banner. LGBT+ communities require people to hold an unshakable set of beliefs, and yet they celebrate personalized identities within those parameters. Where this succeeds, there is unity and diversity. It works because it's capitalizing on elements from the communal nature of God and Christianity.

God and Christianity Are All About Community

God is communal. He is the *triune* God—Father, Son, and Holy Spirit. Everything God does he does in community. Each member of the Trinity belongs to the others, and they all act in perfect unison. The most mind-bending reality of Christianity is that God invites us into this community. Not as a doorman or employee but as a son, a daughter, a spouse. Jesus' prayer is that we might know this and really believe it—that God the Father loves us the way he loves his own Son (John 17:23).

Community is the place where you fulfill your identity and become your best self. It's the environment where you both be and become. This is why family is so important. It should be your first community and biologically the deepest community you will ever have. In a healthy family, you're accepted as you are. You're loved for no other reason than because you're in the family. But a healthy family also helps you become mature. Your parents expect that by the time you're fifteen, they're not still tying your shoes and pouring your Cheerios. They expect that you will become a more mature version of your self, while still being unconditionally part of the family. Of course, they'll keep loving you even if you are still wearing Velcro shoes at fifteen, but their desire is for you to grow.

It's not by accident that people recently have begun referring to their close friends as their "fam." We need formational community, whether we get it from a nuclear family or somewhere else. Our real sticking point—the reason why we can't seem to find this kind of community—is that we don't like to allow other people a say in who we become. The challenge of family is that family should challenge you. But as soon as we feel that happening, it sets off alarm bells in defense of our radically self-constructed identity.

God has given us the church to be our spiritual formational family. Not that it always is, but it should be. We are to "love one another with brotherly affection" and "outdo one another in showing honor" (Romans 12:10). Romans 12 and 1 Corinthians 12 picture the church family as a body in which we are "members one of another." A body needs one organizing executive organ to hold together all the rest of the members. Your brain makes sure, for instance, that your hand works to feed your mouth to chew your food to go to your stomach to then provide energy for the whole thing. In this church-family body, Jesus is the head.

In this body your submission to Jesus also demands that you submit to and serve the other members. "The eye cannot say to the hand, 'I have no need of you'" (1 Corinthians 12:21). Your eye would cease to have any function without all the other parts of the body first enabling it to see and then using the information your eye sends back. In the same way, your spiritual life ceases to function without other people enabling you and then using what you bring to the table. If you try to opt out of the church body, you amputate yourself and handicap the rest of the body.

To address our loneliness crisis, we've got to begin by brushing aside the myth of self-created identity. The truth is that you can only know your self through community. Relationships don't get in the way of self-discovery; they're the best pathway toward it.

There are plenty of communities that provide outside perspective, but the church has something different. It offers something more than that friend you've had since first grade, or a book club, because it reinforces some capital-T Truths about your identity: You're created by God. You're a sinner in need of forgiveness. As you surrender your life to Jesus, he transforms you into your best self.

Community Helps You See Yourself as You Really Are

There's a time when King David hits a real low, and God sends a friend to pick him up (1 Samuel 23:14-18). David's been on the run from Saul, living in caves and in the wilderness. He's exhausted and discouraged. God's promise that he will be king seems like a distant memory. His best friend, Jonathan, seeks him out in the wilderness and encourages him: "Do not fear, for the hand of Saul my father shall not find you. You shall be king over Israel" (v 17). God often uses other people to build your strength and remind you of his purposes. In God's family, you have the privilege of both receiving and giving exhortations and encouragements.

In my final year of college, I lived in a suite with five other guys. Some of us had been friends since freshman year. For a Halloween party, we decided that each of us would dress up as someone else from the suite and act "in character." When each of us saw these caricatures of ourselves, we all had the same reaction: "Come on, that's not me!" Of course everyone was exaggerating their chosen person's style and irritating habits. But interestingly, everybody else felt like the costume and characterization was on point. That's because other people see us a lot better than we see ourselves, especially when it comes to sins and weaknesses.

Many years later, all of us have fond memories of that party. Nobody was actually offended, despite being made fun of. I came away with a better sense of how I was being seen. That kind of revelation was only made possible because of the relationships that already existed. Our guards were down because we felt safe and comfortable with each other. You knew you were loved despite the flaws your friend was highlighting. That's part of what's valuable about the family of God.

But how many of our relationships ever get there? When you get married or start dating someone seriously, that's the kind of relationship you're signing up for. But we need more than one person to tell us the truth about ourselves. And even in those committed relationships, people often cut the conversation off when it gets confrontational. Our culture teaches the perverse idea that as soon as someone criticizes you, that person is toxic. Unfortunately, there are toxic things in *you* that you'll never see without a thick, trusted community. God has given us the local church to be that thick community. It's a group of people meant to help each other become who God has made them to be.

Church, Community, and Confession

The blessing in the explosion of therapy in the past twenty years is that we've become much more comfortable acknowledging weakness. The problem is that secular mental-health solutions often fail to go deep enough. Unless you have the solution of Jesus' infinite redemption ready at hand, it's just too painful if you go too deep. But if you never fix the slanted and crumbling foundation of your self, you'll never be able to build very high. You must acknowledge that you are a sinner—you have to see yourself the way God sees you but saves you anyway—before you can *become* who you're meant to be.

In *Life Together*, Dietrich Bonhoeffer's classic work on Christian community, he explains:

> *The greatest psychological insight, ability, and experience cannot grasp this one thing: what sin is ... Only the Christian knows this. In the presence of a psychiatrist I can only be a sick man; in the presence of a Christian brother I can dare to be a sinner.*[36]

It is only in church that you can dare to be a sinner—that is, dare to be a full human being. As you sit weekly under the preaching of the gospel, God's word acts like a sword, piercing "to the division ... of joints and of marrow, and discerning the thoughts and intentions of the heart" (Hebrews 4:12). God's word pierces you to heal you and build you up. Church brings you into something you can't get from a therapy session. It's not a "you problem"; it's a "we problem." We are convicted together, confess together, and receive grace together. After starting there, we can share our specific struggles that come on top of that. A healthy church provides a community of people who can help you see yourself truly (including your sin) and grow into who you should be (through repentance).

Help Church Achieve Its Potential

I have a good friend; we'll call him Steve. God has radically transformed Steve's life. He connects several times a week with his recovery group and a therapist. He also attends his church's worship service and Bible studies. These are all great things, but there's a sad question that keeps plaguing me: why does he need so many resources *outside* the church?

I don't mean to diminish the value of recovery groups or therapy. Just the opposite. But these things are so valuable, so normal, so reflexively sought after outside of the church because there is something missing inside the church: we don't normalize confession and forgiveness. These practices provide a beautiful opportunity for the church to serve as the healing community God intends for it to be.

Churches can build into their worship and small groups a cultural expectation that people who attend there are sinners who need ongoing forgiveness and healing. Whether you've grown up in a church community or are coming to one for the first time, you need to be driving toward one thing: relationships where you can confess and receive forgiveness.

I'm not saying you shouldn't be in communities outside the church; I'm saying the church has tremendous potential woven into its DNA to act as your most important community. Every good, healthy community you've been a part of is good precisely because it's drawing on something the church should be.

The church is an eternal family whose members are connected through the spiritual bloodlines of Jesus' sacrifice. It is an oasis in a world of catfishing and ghosting people online. It's a place to share your identity, not curate it. It's a place where you can dare to *be* a sinner *becoming* more fully redeemed.

Confession Is Fertilizer

Your pride acts like a gravitational pull inward, away from confession and community. Pride makes you think, "I have a right to my self, my hatred and my desires, my life and my death ... [therefore] confession in the presence of a brother is the profoundest kind of humiliation."[37]

Humiliation lands on us as something entirely negative, even horrific. We imagine humiliation as people pointing and laughing while we do something along the lines of giving a speech with no pants. There is, however, a cathartic and transformative humiliation in which you expose parts of your inner self that you wish were not the way they are to another person. It's humiliating because you don't *want* to be that way. The other person sees you in a way that you don't even like to see yourself, then responds with an acceptance that you can't seem to grant yourself.

Humiliation, then, is actually the doorway into thick community, which is why the latter is so rare. As the apostle John says, "If we walk in the light [he clarifies in the following verses that this means confessing], as he is in the light, we have fellowship with one another, and the blood of Jesus his Son cleanses us from all sin (1 John 1:7).

Our sinful wiring leads us to hide and deceive when it comes to our sin (John 3:19). We figure, *If other people knew this, they wouldn't accept me.* To some degree, that fear is well founded. Community has layers, and peeling back layers takes time and effort. You don't invite someone you just met to go on vacation with you. Too much too soon. But think about how you feel when a trusted friend shares about her long-term struggle with body image and food. You're drawn in, not repulsed, by that. Your heart is warmed and softened toward your friend. You have a newfound respect for her bravery. We gain dignity when we're willing to lay it down. When you dig into your sin and weakness, you have more to offer in relationships, not less. One of God's primary goals in your suffering and sin is that, down the road, you will be able to turn around and "comfort those who are in any affliction, with the comfort with which we ourselves are comforted by God" (2 Corinthians 1:4).

The way you receive supernatural help and become your best self is by acknowledging your neediness: "Therefore I will boast all the more gladly of my weaknesses, so that the power of Christ may rest upon me" (2 Corinthians 12:9). The Bible presents an upside-down secret weapon—strength through weakness. The more you see and confess sin, the more grace and forgiveness you receive—from God and others. The more you receive grace and forgiveness, the more you are experiencing a supernatural power, rather than trying to tap the weary well of your own willpower.

Dietrich Bonhoeffer, who had to find his Christian community in secret under Nazi Germany, learned to prize confession—the more specific, the better:

> *A man who confesses his sins in the presence of a brother knows that he is no longer alone with himself; he experiences the presence of God in the reality of the other person ... Mutual, brotherly confession is given to us by God in order that we may be sure of divine forgiveness. But it is precisely for the sake of this certainty that confession should deal with concrete sins.*[38]

You don't have generic problems, and you won't experience real community generically. You're angry with your girlfriend, Olivia, because she doesn't like your friend Brian. You share that specific problem and confess that specific anger to one of your specific friends, James. James listens sympathetically and reminds you of the grace and forgiveness of Jesus. Before you know it, you are experiencing deeper community with James than ninety percent of people will ever know.

To Become Bigger You Need to Immerse Yourself in Something Bigger

So far, the reasons to value church community are these:

1. You are created for community both with God and with others.
2. The church helps you see who you really are and become your best self through confession, forgiveness, and God's grace.

The last reason you need church is because it brings the truest experience of something God has made all of us to want: communal transcendence.

The way you become your best self is by plugging into something bigger than yourself. People do this in solitary ways, like looking up at the night sky or losing themselves in the vastness of nature. But we also seek this kind of experience through what we could call communal liturgies of transcendence.

This is why people pay good money to go to sporting events, concerts, and political rallies.[39] You could sit at home by yourself and watch a game or listen to music or digest politics, but that's not the point. The *atmosphere* is the point. You're swept up into a greater cause. You see, hear, and feel a unifying experience of transcendence. Your sense of self is enhanced, not diminished, as you lose yourself in a crowd of people who are all attached to something bigger than themselves on their own.

God wants us to experience this communal transcendence when we worship together at church. It's one of the reasons why online services can't replace the real thing. You find freedom and clarity as an individual as you give yourself up to a collective which, in turn, is given up to God—the most transcendent being in the world.

My suggestion when it comes to finding a church community is: don't make it complicated. No church is perfect. Find a church where they focus on Jesus, teach the Bible, and love each other through confession and forgiveness. As you immerse yourself in this community over a long-term commitment, you will find your *self* expanding. You will be like a triangle, drawn upward and outward by all three corners at once. You become a bigger version of your self as you move upward toward God and outward toward other people.

Questions for Discussion and Reflection

1. How have you seen people's values and identity shaped by the community they're in? How has this happened for you?
2. Do you have a good friend who's also willing to call you out when needed? Why are those friendships so hard to develop?
3. Why do you think someone confessing their weakness or failure tends to strengthen that relationship? What can you do in your local church to encourage this practice more?

CHAPTER 9

Three Red Herrings: Work, Sex, and Politics

I saved this chapter for last because I want to practice what I preach. We spend way too much time and energy defining identity in terms of what we're *not*, without bothering to ponder who we *should* be. Now that we've seen what a biblical identity journey *does* look like—becoming more of who you are in Christ—the time has come to mark some Xs at the trailheads of some of the world's most enticing alternatives.

In mystery and detective stories, red herrings are false clues—dead-ends that look convincingly important. You start drawing certain conclusions and solidifying assumptions as you chase the red herring, which turns out to be completely false. Many times, the pursuit wastes valuable time, and the detective has to go back to the drawing board. I want to save you that time.

Three powerful alternatives that our world offers as master identities are work, sexuality, and politics. The digital media platform you spend the most time on might cue you in to which one you find most compelling—

LinkedIn and email (for work), Instagram (for sexuality), and X and Facebook (for politics).

These three are identity categories large enough to give you a sense of both being and becoming. But they are red herrings. I want to examine how each one offers a potential master identity, how this falls short, and why these spheres of life should serve us only as sub-identities under a Christian's Jesus-focused master identity. They are legitimate parts of who we are—they don't need to be thrown out altogether—but they do need to be stewarded well. You will see how doing that can actually help you in the process of becoming your Jesus-self.

Work

Your work, or more precisely your hoped-for vocation, offers a place for you to be and become. Let's say, for example, you *are* a nurse. That's part of your being. You also love what you do as a nurse (an affinity)—helping others, supporting them, offering care in time of crisis. Because it's such an important part of your identity, you want to *become* the best nurse you can be.

Henry Ford, the great entrepreneur of the assembly line, proclaimed that "thinking men know that work is the salvation of the race, morally, physically, socially. Work does more than get us a living; it gets us a life."[40] When people speak about vocation, you'll start to hear overt spiritual words like these—talk of a higher purpose, a sense of calling, a path to transcendence and even immortality if you achieve something remarkable.

In the twenty-first century, some of us are cursed with the blessing of greatly expanded vocational options. The internet is always an arm's length away, glistening like a virtual goldrush. Sociologists predict that young adults entering the workforce today will have five or more careers (complete with all the joys of being fired and retrained along the way).[41]

The pressure of all these potential opportunities leaves you with a constant sense that you're settling for second-best. *Is there something better out there?* you wonder. *Perhaps some currently undiscovered career that I could define for myself—one that would unite all my skills, passions, and personality into one wildly profitable and fulfilling destiny?*

It's easy to spin out a narrative of identity around your work. Identity is your sense of self that connects who you are as a product of your past with who you wish to be in the future. Work hands you a ready-made mold for doing that.

Work as identity affirms where you are today (you're gaining experience, paying your dues), and it always holds out something greater for your future (the best is yet to come). The problem, of course, is that this is very fragile. Tomorrow your company could go under, or you could get fired. Finding your identity in what you do rather than who you are in Jesus devalues your worth. We all want to feel we are contributing in a meaningful way, but a shelf in your pantry contributes in a meaningful way. You are more than the sum of your executed functions. Even when you're crushing it at your job, work as identity is a tease. The only way you move upward is by being restlessly *dis*content with life as it currently is—the less content you are, the more you're striving, and the better your odds of moving up.

JOSEPH SHOWS US HOW TO STEWARD VOCATION

The story of Joseph (Genesis 37 – 50) gives us a picture of how to steward vocational skills while basing your identity on God, not vocation. God gifts Joseph with high competency in two skills: dream interpretation and business management. These skills are not one-time divine interventions but patterns of gifting that Joseph stewards in service to God throughout his life.

It would have been easy, when he was sold as a slave, for Joseph to shut down. But his master, an Egyptian officer named Potiphar, sees Joseph's business management skills at work and promotes him. Still, Joseph could have chosen to harbor resentment and do the bare minimum. Why should he pour out his best—his ingenuity, energy, and talents—for this foreign slaveowner? But Joseph doesn't think this way. Instead he stewards his God-given vocational skills wherever he is. "From the time that he [Potiphar] made him overseer in his house and over all that he had, the LORD blessed the Egyptian's house for Joseph's sake" (Genesis 39:5).

What do you do if you find yourself working for a boss who doesn't respect you, in a role where you're underutilized, unappreciated and underpaid? Maybe you find a new job. But in the meantime, you steward and sharpen the skills God has given you to excel in the work you do have.

After a while, Joseph's success puts him in harm's way. Potiphar's wife takes an interest in him. When Joseph doesn't respond the way she wants, he is entrapped, falsely accused, and thrown in jail (v 7-20). Now Joseph will give up, right? Just stop trying. Let it all burn. No—he goes back to work. "The keeper of the prison put Joseph in charge of all the prisoners who were in the prison. Whatever was done there, he was the one who did it" (v 22). It takes a special work of God for someone to land in a prison the way Joseph did, then look around and say,

"Okay, how can I help out here? How can I steward my skills in this environment?"

Maybe you're working right now in a context you find less than ideal. Unless your profession itself is patently sinful, the most important thing for you today is to see both your context and your skills as God-given, then do what you can to help.

After Joseph spends several years of largely thankless labor in prison, his vocational faithfulness gets him recommended to Pharaoh. After interpreting Pharaoh's dream, Joseph offers his management advice (41:33-36). Joseph is still stewarding his vocational skills in every opportunity. Finally, God reveals his plan for Joseph's faithful service when Pharaoh puts Joseph in charge of managing the largest empire in the known world. Joseph is ready for that calling when it comes because he never stopped stewarding his gifts to serve the Lord, regardless of his circumstances.

Work and vocation are blessings from the Lord. In our work, we're meant to imitate and reflect God's wise and beautiful work. But the way to become your best self isn't by loading your identity onto the roller coaster of career. You pursue your best self by becoming like Jesus. In that pursuit you harness your vocational gifts and skills in every environment, at all times.

Let's say you have a passion for art and you work at a medical office. Are there ways you can steward your art vocation to bring beauty to the office or the company's web presence? In doing so, you're harnessing your vocational gift to showcase God's beauty in your current context. "So, whether you eat or drink, or whatever you do, do all to the glory of God" (1 Corinthians 10:31). Some environments *appear* more significant than others, but becoming like Jesus has nothing to do with significant environments. It has to do with your relationship with God in any environment.

Sexuality

Whatever sexual inclination you feel, there are people eager to affirm that as the *primary* thing that defines you. Much of a person's sexuality has to do with perception—with feelings of attraction or attractiveness. Sex is a culmination of these feelings, but sexuality is far bigger than merely a sex act.

The appeal of sexuality as a master identity is that it offers you a place to be and to become. This is a rather new development. People have always had various sexual attractions, but before the last sixty or seventy years, these feelings were pretty low on the identity food chain, compared with things like religion, family, and tribe.

Today, your sexual inclination can place you in a group of people where you belong—a place where everyone else shares that type of attraction. Over time, you assimilate into the narrative of that group, which explains life through this particular sexual orientation.

In his book *Understanding Sexual Identity,* Mark Yarhouse, a professor at Wheaton College who specializes in the intersection of religious and sexual identity, lays out some chief tenets of a gay-identity narrative:

- *Same-sex attractions reflect* ***real differences*** *between people, not just behavior choices.*
- *These attractions accurately signal* ***who you are*** *as a person.*

- *Your attractions reside at the core of* ***your identity****, your sense of self.*
- *If you are Gay (as an identity), it makes sense to follow through and act on what you feel (your attractions)—because you are expressing and enjoying who you are.*

[Causes of being gay]:

You are born Gay—it's just a matter of discovering this about yourself.

If you have same-sex attractions but don't identify as Gay, then you're in denial or not yet ready to be honest with yourself about who you are.[42]

This script is not a doctrinal manifesto that you read, sign, and pin to your wall, but one that emerges through the narratives of those who subscribe to it. As people in this identity group tell their story, it gives others in the group a set of shared beliefs and values to adhere to and then to articulate in their own stories. One of the core beliefs at play here is that your sexuality (being gay) *must* reside at the core of your identity.

Let's say Andrew is the father of three teenagers and has been married to Hannah for twenty-three years. In the past five years, he and Hannah have drifted apart. He's developed feelings for his friend Daniel, which led to a sexual encounter. Now he's begun rethinking all his former male friendships. Within a gay-identity script, it doesn't matter what complex feelings Andrew might have for Hannah—many in today's culture would say it would be inauthentic for Andrew to go back and work on their marriage.

Sexuality becomes a master identity when it takes on spiritual overtones. It explains and provides meaning for your life. This can happen for what culture calls a hetero cisgendered man (a straight guy who believes he's a guy) just as much as for a polyamorous transgender woman (a man who believes he's a woman and has multiple sexual partners). With sexuality as a master identity, everything and everyone acts either for or against your sexual identity. This is how you will view the terrain in your journey of becoming. You have an aim—a goal to fight for: the free development of your sexuality. There's no clear end to this journey (see chapter 4), but it is a way to be and become. Supposedly, you can discover your best self through an evolving expression of your sexuality.

The great sadness of every sort of mistaken master identity is that it hollows you out. This is perhaps nowhere more obvious than in sexuality. You're trying to force the weight of your soul into a particular wavelength of *feeling*. You're trying to define yourself chiefly by your experience and pursuit of attraction.

This is dangerous territory indeed. Feelings of attraction are ephemeral, open to interpretation, and not something to base your identity around. You can make choices about how you cultivate and express a feeling. You can place boundaries around what you do or don't do with it. We all have to interpret and prioritize our feelings into the larger vision of the identity we wish to become. It's not a matter of denying a feeling; it's a matter of channeling that feeling in the appropriate direction.

Sexuality as identity is simply not enough. Your identity is meant to be based on a relationship with God. Identifying yourself by a sexual orientation takes one kind of feeling and makes it the most important thing about you. You lose sight of the richness and complexity of your humanity.

STEWARDING YOUR SEXUALITY

Regardless of your relationship status, keeping Jesus at the center of your identity will provide a focal direction for stewarding your sexuality at every stage of life. After all, sexuality is a gift from God, meant to point us toward intimacy with God when used within the good limits God prescribes (Genesis 2:24; 1 Corinthians 7:9).

In 1 Corinthians 7, Paul presents a theology of singleness to a hypersexualized culture who viewed sex either like water (the more the better) or, in reaction, saw it as shameful and base—to be avoided as much as possible. In truth, it's neither. Neither marriage (and sex) nor singleness (and celibacy) provide a superior track toward self-transformation (1 Corinthians 7:25-31). Each has its pros and cons. Within each you gain certain opportunities and miss out on others. In other words, your sexuality, whether experienced in the bounds of marriage or singleness, works a lot like every other part of your identity. You're meant to make the best use of it in your circumstances today to serve the Lord. "Let each person lead the life that the Lord has assigned to him, and to which God has called him" (1 Corinthians 7:17).

Let's think through a few examples. What if you're a married man experiencing same-sex attraction? Start by committing to God's parameters for expressing your sexuality—within your marriage. Work to deepen both your friendship with your wife and healthy friendships with other men. There's much joy, wisdom, and support you can gain by male friendships that come through non-sexualized channels. God is growing you through helping you to see these other men as God does.

What if you're a single woman struggling with lust? Start by recognizing God's appropriate outlet for that desire—within the context of a marriage. Strive to become your best self in Jesus now, and if you are looking for a husband, search for a partner doing the same thing. In the meantime, channel your unfulfilled sexual energy and riches of surplus time into serving others—in your work, in ministry opportunities, or in building deep relationships. Memorize Psalm 16:11: "You make known to me the path of life. In your presence there is fullness of joy; at your right hand are pleasures forevermore."

What if you're a married man who is feeling sexually unfulfilled? Once again, start by committing to God's parameters for expressing your sexuality—within your marriage. Steward your sexuality by developing your friendship with your wife. See and love her as God does. Offer your unfulfilled desires to God, who withholds "no good thing… from those who walk uprightly" (Psalm 84:11). Embrace the intimacy of suffering with Christ as he meets your desires and reorders your perspective.

Most importantly for our culture today, stewarding your sexuality, just like stewarding your health, means you don't let it take over. "'Food is meant for the stomach and the stomach for food'—and God will destroy both one and the other. The body is not meant for sexual immorality, but for the Lord, and the Lord for the body" (1 Corinthians 6:13). If your life is about more than muscle tone or finding the perfect pizza, then it's also about more than sexuality.

Don't hollow out the richness of your identity by fixating on this one sub-identity. You are and do a lot of things that have very little (if anything) to do with sex. If you make your identity with Jesus your master identity, your sexuality will fall into its rightful place: contributing to your pursuit of your best self rather than being the pursuit. You will be able to steward your sexuality in a way that leads you and others to know and enjoy God better.

Politics

Among the various secular master identities, politics perhaps offers the most compelling hope of communal transcendence. It promises a higher cause that will take you to a higher plateau of life. This higher cause comes with the complete package of a value system, creed, worldview, and hope for salvation—if only enough people will join your side.

Because of that, politics can comfortably take up the throne of master identity. You choose to be a member of the "correct" political group and tribe. You can become more of a faithful follower and leader of this cause. You proselytize, campaign, and give your life to this identity, all "in service of others," because your political system offers the solution the world needs. It's a counterfeit gospel that gains power by saying it serves the greater good. This is one reason why so many people "mature" into caring more about politics as they get older. It supposedly centers your identity on the higher cause of serving society.

But two problems arise when you put politics at the center of your identity: disillusionment and tribal violence.

DISILLUSIONMENT

Politics promises that the pathway to identity fulfillment is for your side to win and gain more power. But it doesn't really offer a clear path for dealing with defeat, so it often leads to disillusionment. Usually, you're left concluding that people are in fact more stupid, selfish, backward, or cruel than you'd hoped they were. Do you really want to keep fighting, keep pouring out your life to help *those kinds* of people?

Even when your side wins, disillusionment sets in, perhaps worse than in the losses. Things don't change as much as you'd like them to. The leaders you put your hope in compromise or fail. Those dunces on the other side refuse to see reason. The great political vision your identity has been wrapped up in crumbles into theatrics and backbiting.

Either way, a focus on political identity proves insufficient. You then grow older with a growing disillusionment—a growing sense that you will never see the only thing you've given yourself to see. A nagging question grows bigger and bigger with each passing decade: *What has this all been for? I'm nearing the end of my life and things feel worse now than ever. Maybe, you start thinking, the only answer is to crush the other side completely—to force them into what's good for them.* This brings us to the second problem.

TRIBAL VIOLENCE

Centering your identity on politics brings you into a zero-sum game where might makes right. Because the stakes are so high, producing a winning result can justify all kinds of shady maneuvers. Your moral compass gets co-opted by your tribe. Did someone from your tribe cheat on his wife? *Well, no one's perfect, and we don't know the whole story.* Did someone from the other tribe hire one of her friends? *That's because she's a corrupt dictator who surrounds herself with spineless suck-ups.*

Politics works powerfully as a master identity because it not only gives you your sense of self; it also gives you categories to interpret everything else around you. The world becomes more black-and-white, which makes it easier for you to make decisions and evaluations. Most people have enough restraint (or maybe it's only cowardice) to not engage in physical violence, but political identity will at least result in psychological violence. Your mind and heart become more hardened to *those people*, whom you find more and more incomprehensible.

Over time, this posture of political violence corrodes your heart. Your tribe becomes smaller, and its list of enemies grows longer. It's no longer merely the people on the other side of the spectrum who have earned your disdain; it's also the people with whom you once agreed but who have now compromised or grown soft. Since your hope is in political power, this is a real downer. The smaller your tribe becomes, the more vocal and vicious you must become to make sure you're not trampled on. Or you go back to the first problem—disillusionment and depression.

THE POLITICS OF JESUS' KINGDOM

In Matthew 16:16-20, in response to Jesus' question "Who do you say that I am?" Peter says, "You are the Christ." *Great job*, Jesus says (paraphrased). But then directly afterward, as Jesus begins explaining that his mission is to suffer and die, Peter takes Jesus aside to rebuke him about this plan. Jesus responds to Peter by calling him "Satan."

What's going on here?

Peter has grasped Jesus' identity, but his pathway *to* power—through suffering and dying—makes no sense at all. We can't blame Peter. Jesus' brothers had the same trouble. They said to Jesus, "If you do these things [miraculous signs], show yourself to the world" (John 7:4). In other words, if your identity really is the Son of God—if you really have these powers—start showing them off! Make a spectacle. Build your tribe.

Both Peter and Jesus' brothers are scratching their heads because they can grasp Jesus' final destination (power and glory) but not the road he's taking to get there (the cross). The same road should be true for his followers today. Politics as a desire to improve and to build up society is a beautiful thing. But if you are becoming your Jesus-self, you will take Jesus' path to get to that goal—a path of personal suffering and sacrifice. The results speak for themselves. Two thousand years after Jesus spoke those words to Peter, every other kingdom and empire in history has fallen except the one that Jesus is building. He builds it through his disciples taking up their cross and following him (Matthew 16:24-26).

Jesus' second-greatest commandment to his disciples is to love your neighbor as yourself (Mark 12:31). Even when you make following Jesus your master identity, politics (or cultural engagement) is still important because it's looking to benefit others. The correct master identity of Jesus simply changes the approach. A Christian approach to politics is about stewarding your community engagement. You are a member of many communities: your family, neighborhood, city, state or province, and country. You should care about all these communities.

Stewardship helps you prioritize your community responsibilities. Unless you're a foreign ambassador, your words and actions will have a much bigger impact on your family than on the people of Madagascar. Therefore, you have a more pressing responsibility to steward your role in the community of your family than to steward your country's foreign relations. You will do far more political good getting to know your neighbor than staying up to speed on the scandal of your state representative. You will find more fulfillment stewarding the values of Jesus with one coworker than with dozens of strangers online. Opportunities to steward community involvement as an outflow of your identity present themselves all the time. But these look much different than what often passes for political engagement.

I'm not saying you shouldn't read the news, talk politics, vote, volunteer for a campaign, or run for office. But Christians should steward their political engagement according to the communities God has already placed them in. First consider the places where you are already being and becoming. These are the communities where you have the greatest opportunity to accomplish the real goal of politics—benefiting others.

Diversify Your Identity Portfolio

Think of your multiple identities like an investment portfolio. When you make Jesus your master identity, it's like signing up for an expertly managed index fund. Jesus will perfectly balance all the other parts of your identity to serve the one goal of becoming more of who he's made you to be—your Jesus-self.

The trouble with these three red herrings of identity (as well as others not mentioned here) is that they produce an unbalanced life. They overconcentrate your identity in one stock, so to speak. You're subsequently exposed to high levels of risk, violent fluctuations, and ultimately bankruptcy.

Work, sexuality, and politics are all legitimate parts of your identity. But if you make any one of them your master identity, you become one-dimensional and miss the fullness of life God has for you in Jesus. If, on the other hand, you have Jesus at the center, becoming like him will lead you to steward your sub-identities for his glory and transform you into what really is your best self.

Questions for Discussion and Reflection

1. Why does a work identity promise so much fulfillment? How can you steward your giftings in the work God has put before you right now?
2. What kinds of difficulties can come from centering too much of your identity on a feeling—sexual or otherwise?
3. Do you tend more towards political frustration or disillusionment? Why? How can you steward your community engagement?

CONCLUSION

How You Become Who You Are

I love productivity books. They're all about becoming your best self. They tap into this core desire we have—not merely a desire for efficiency in itself, as if you're a machine being tuned up to pump out more bottle caps, but a desire to care well for your *self*. You want to *become*—not a different person altogether but a better, more focused version of you: the kind of person who more consistently lives up to who you want to be.

The whole field of self-help (perhaps the fastest growing pseudo-religion in the West) orbits around the question: how do you become your best self? How do you unlock the potential that you feel you must surely have within, and grow into what you might become? The goal of self-improvement trades on an older, better, more robust Christian goal: sanctification.

The aim of this book has been to recast our world's quest for self-actualization into a clearer, more satisfying biblical vision. The verse that crystallizes this biblical journey is 2 Corinthians 3:18: "We all, with unveiled face, beholding the glory of the Lord, are being transformed into the same image from one degree of glory to another."

The Bible gives you an infinitely more stable vision of your best self than our world, because it's an image that has never and will never change—Jesus Christ. When you give your life to Jesus, he begins working out this process of sanctification inside you. Through his Spirit, you are being transformed into more and more and more of your best self.

But what's your part in this? How can you get more of this transformation? Is there any way you can accelerate the process? There is. And we find it in one of the few places where this same Greek word for "transform" shows up: "Do not be conformed to this world, but be transformed by the renewal of your mind" (Romans 12:2).

People talk about books or movies transforming their lives. That happens. But only if you keep thinking about them. Keep revisiting them. Keep letting their ideas shape your life. That's what you need to do to transform. And for the record, I'm not talking about this book transforming you; I'm talking about the Bible. The activity of "beholding the Lord" (2 Corinthians 3:18), which transforms you from one state of glory to the next, is not some mystic vision or state of flow or spiritual mountain ascended only by supersaints. It's about the renewal of your mind through God's word.

The passivity of Romans 12:2 is both humbling and encouraging. It's humbling because you never escape this process of being shaped. You are either *being* conformed to this world or you're *being* transformed by the renewal of your mind. In other words, your person, your self, is never merely acting. Your self is also always being *acted upon*. Even when you are most energetically putting yourself out there (and perhaps especially then), your self is still being shaped.

The process of being sanctified is not just about turning off the TV or getting off your phone, as important as those things may be. You need to realize that whether you are being frenetically productive or lounging in the company of a good friend, your mind is being shaped. This isn't a bad thing; it's simply how God has made us.

This passivity should also be encouraging because the bar is low in some ways. Becoming your best self can be as simple as putting yourself in the right "places." I'm not talking so much about physical places as mental ones. What contexts and influences are shaping your mind right now? Who are the people you look up to? What values and aspirations are you exposing your mind to most often? Romans 12:2 teaches us that your mind is like the eye of your identity. Remember:

Identity is your sense of self
that connects who you are as a product of your past
with who you wish to be in the future.

Your mind is lighting the path of your identity journey. How do you make sense of your past? Who is the person you see yourself growing into? But your mind is never operating in isolation. It's always being conformed or transformed by the contexts you place it in. If you immerse your mind in beholding Jesus, you will have a stable context, a stable vision, and therefore a stable identity—even as you continue to grow.

The thesis of how a Christian becomes his or her best self is simple: Jesus and the Holy Spirit through God's word among God's people will transform your mind and self into someone more glorious than you could imagine. This also makes Christian identity formation all-encompassing. You need to expose yourself to those transforming powers as often as you can.

There's nothing I can say about the practical steps of sanctification that you can't already guess. That's because there's nothing earth-shaking about how identity transformation happens. Every person decides the master identity that will be most important to him or her. Then he or she simply becomes more of that. The *becoming* of an identity happens right alongside the deciding on or the cherishing of that identity.

For a Christian, that means you decide that being a Christian is the most important thing about you. You want to become more of that. You should therefore seek out the contexts that will transform your mind. Read your Bible. Pray. Join a local church. Immerse yourself in thick Christian friendships where you are known and loved and you know and love others. Download and listen to sermons. Read classic Christian books on identity formation like Augustine's *Confessions* or J.I. Packer's *Knowing God*. Memorize Scripture. Tuck those verses away and meditate on them.

All of these activities are ways in which you expose your mind to the transforming power and grace of Jesus. The more you do these things, the faster you'll see the transformation happening (1 Timothy 4:12-15).

Let me close by repeating one final word of advice on being transformed. Humility. You have to want to be transformed by Jesus. That means being willing to be confronted, challenged, and stretched. If you approach any of the above sanctification practices, even subconsciously, as a way of seeking tools to advance your own reputation or power, you will be transformed... but in an entirely different direction. If, however, you approach these practices as a Christian seeking to behold Jesus, you will find yourself becoming who you are—your truest and best self. Your Jesus-self.

Acknowledgments

Shortly before we got married, my wife, Liz, supported transitioning my ThM studies into a DMin., little knowing all that it would mean. She cared for our family and home, often while someone was just getting sick, while I left to do week-long intensive classes that built the body of research I used for this book. She has sustained and strengthened my writing throughout our marriage. She's also developed my self-awareness more than any other person. I'm so grateful for how God has used her as an identity-transforming partner.

My parents have encouraged and supported my studies since I was a child, and have continued doing so all the way through seminary and doctoral work. I'm grateful for all the formational givens God has gifted me through the way they brought me up. Most of all, I'm grateful for their example, and that of my brother Ransom, of steadfastly centering their identities on Jesus and teaching me to do the same.

Thanks to my good friend Byron West and the leadership of Westminster PCA in Fort Myers and All Saints PCA in Boise, who supported my doctoral work and writing.

The congregation at graciously served as my guinea pigs in testing out many of the practical applications of these identity lessons.

I'm deeply grateful for Shelton Woods, a founding elder of All Saints Presbyterian, who has been a fan and first-round editor of all my writing for several years.

This book owes its life in print to Katy Morgan, an editor at The Good Book Company. Katy championed the potential in this book when no one else did and walked me through crafting rough ideas into something someone might actually want to read. She and Maggie Combs, who came in as another set of eyes, made this book become its best self.

I'm indebted to many writers and professors I've stolen from along the way, not least of which are my father, Vern Poythress, and one of my professors, Carl Trueman. They cast a compelling vision of biblical identity in a world of confusion.

Finally, I'm grateful for my daughters, Eleanor and Sophia Grace, who have already shaped my identity more than they will ever know. I pray God, as their true Father, grows them into everything he's made them to become.

Endnotes

1 Brian Rosner, *How to Find Yourself: Why Looking Inward Is Not the Answer* (Crossway, 2022), p. 34.

2 Brian Rosner, *How to Find Yourself*, p. 34.

3 David Brooks, *The Road to Character* (Random House, 2015), p. 63.

4 Carl Trueman, *The Rise and Triumph of the Modern Self* (Crossway, 2020), p. 39.

5 Brian Rosner, *How to Find Yourself*, p. 16.

6 John Frame, *A History of Western Philosophy and Theology* (P&R, 2015), p. 65.

7 Irenaeus, Adv. Haer. 4.20.7, trans. Philip Schaff, www.ccel.org/ccel/schaff/anf01.html, p. 818.

8 Paul Barnett, *Second Epistle to the Corinthians* (William B. Eerdmans Publishing Company, 1997), p. 205-206.

9 Jan Lambrecht, "Transformation in 2 Cor 3:18" in *Biblica Vol. 64 (2)*, 1983, p. 250.

10 A character who is clearly Enneagram 7 or a Myers-Briggs ESTP.

11 Timothy Keller, *Preaching: Communicating Faith in an Age of Skepticism* (Penguin, 2015), p. 136.

12 Paul E. Miller, *A Praying Life: Connecting with God in a Distracted World* (NavPress, 2017), p. 258.

13 There is a debate about whether Paul is referring here to life before or after becoming a Christian. I believe it is the latter.

14 Isaiah Berlin, "Two Concepts of Liberty" in *Four Essays on Liberty* (Oxford University Press, 1969), p. 118-172.

15 Michel Foucault, "Afterword: The Subject and Power" in Hubert L. Dreyfus and Paul Rabinow, *Michel Foucault: Beyond Structuralism and Hermeneutics,* 2nd edition (University of Chicago Press, 1983), p. 222.

16 Charles Davis, "Our Modern Identity: The Formation of the Self," *Modern Theology 6* (2) (January 1990), p. 166-7.

17 Isaiah Berlin, "Two Concepts of Liberty", p. 172.

18 Timothy Keller, *Preaching*, p. 144.

19 John Webster, *Confessing God* (Bloomsbury T & T Clark, 2005), p. 224.

20 John Webster, *Confessing God*, p. 225.

21 Twenty One Pilots, "Stressed Out," *Blurryface,* Track 2 (Fueled by Ramen, 2015).

22 This is also why it can be extremely difficult to trust God with that kind of parental responsibility if you never saw it modeled.

23 Jerome Bruner, "Life as Narrative," *Social Research* 71, (3) (Fall 2004), p. 691.

24 Greg Lukianoff and Jonathan Haidt, "The Coddling of the American Mind," *The Atlantic*, September

2015, accessed July 15, 2019, www.theatlantic.com/magazine/archive/2015/09/the-coddling-ofthe-american-mind/399356/.

25 As above.

26 As above.

27 Elevation Worship, "O Come to the Altar (Radio Version)," 2016.

28 John Owen, *Communion with God: Of Communion with God the Father, Son, and Holy Ghost, each person distinctly, in love, grace, and consolation; or, The saints' fellowship with the Father, Son, and Holy Ghost unfolded* (Benediction Classics, 2017), p. 214.

29 As above.

30 Timothy Keller with Kathy Keller, *The Meaning of Marriage: Facing the Complexities of Commitment with the Wisdom of God* (Penguin Books, 2013), p. 120.

31 As above, p. 121.

32 Shirley MacLaine, quoted in Henry Fairlie, *The Seven Deadly Sins Today* (New Republic, 1978), p. 31-32.

33 Jean M. Twenge, *iGen: Why Today's Super-Connected Kids Are Growing Up Less Rebellious, More Tolerant, Less Happy, and Completely Unprepared for Adulthood* (Simon & Schuster, Inc., 2017), p. 215.

34 As above, p. 214.

35 Charles Taylor, *A Secular Age* (Belknap Press, 2007), p. 50.

36 Dietrich Bonhoeffer, *Life Together* (HarperCollins, 1954), p. 119.

37 As above, p. 116.

38 As above, p. 116-17.

39 Charles Taylor, *A Secular Age*, p. 715.

40 Merrill R. Abbey, *Preaching to the Contemporary Mind* (Abingdon Press, 1963), p. 179.

41 Brian Rosner, *How to Find Yourself: Why Looking Inward Is Not the Answer* (Crossway, 2022), p. 44.

42 Mark A. Yarhouse, *Understanding Sexual Identity* (Zondervan, 2013), p. 70.

BIBLICAL | RELEVANT | ACCESSIBLE

At The Good Book Company we are dedicated to helping Christians and local churches grow. We believe that God's growth process always starts with hearing clearly what he has said to us through his timeless and flawless word—the Bible.

Ever since we opened our doors in 1991, we have been striving to produce resources that are biblical, relevant, and accessible. By God's grace, we have grown to become an international publisher, encouraging ordinary Christians of every age and stage and every background and denomination to live for Christ day by day and equipping churches to grow in their knowledge of God, their love for one another, and the effectiveness of their outreach.

Call one of our friendly team for a discussion of your needs or visit one of our local websites for more information on the resources and services we provide.

Your friends at The Good Book Company

"To live in the modern world is to be faced with endless possibilities: to be steeped in ready-made answers to the question, 'Who am I?' This book takes up many of the central questions which all of us face in forming an identity and reframes them by placing Christ at the center. With remarkable warmth, wisdom, and generosity, Justin Poythress encourages readers to embrace a fullness of identity and purpose: a fullness unique to each person, yet one reflecting the fullness of the one who called each of us into being."

KAREN SWALLOW PRIOR, Author, *You Have a Calling*

"*Who Am I and What Am I Doing with My Life?* is a steady and trustworthy revealing of God's answer to the question aglow within each one of us: Who am I? It is deeply wise and pervasively insightful. I will be using this book in my life and ministry."

DANE ORTLUND, Author, *Gentle and Lowly*

"There are few matters more important to young adults than establishing their identity. Yet, in today's culture and climate, there are few matters that are more confusing. Justin Poythress's book will help readers find stability and purpose, not in custom-crafting an identity from the myriad of options available to them but by grounding it firmly and faithfully in the Lord Jesus Christ. This book will prove a trusted guide to anyone who is wrestling through who they are and who God has made them to be."

TIM CHALLIES, Author, *Seasons of Sorrow*

"Engaging, accessible, and biblically faithful. Justin has a pastoral heart and a rooted sense of the real spiritual issues we encounter with our identity. In a culture drowning in expressivism, this book is a life raft. We will only ever know ourselves as we come to know and love Jesus, whose Spirit transforms us into the most beautiful version of ourselves. May this book be a welcome call to daily put on your Jesus-self and put off your sinful self. The more you apply that biblical counsel, the more you will find peace in being yourself: a self for whom God has great purposes and plans."

PIERCE TAYLOR HIBBS, Senior Writer, Westminster Theological Seminary

"Justin Poythress extends a warm invitation to the transforming freedom of immersing ourselves in our master identity in Christ. Gift this title to your favorite aimless twenty-something—but only after you sneak a read yourself."

HOLLY MACKLE, Host, Unseriously podcast

"Justin Poythress is careful in his thinking and full of care for the reader—truthful and gentle and biblical. He deals forthrightly with the felt questions of identity, addressing those matters that weigh on people's hearts and minds, and he does so by constantly turning the reader's attention to biblical truths and invitations. At times this book is uncomfortable because of how it presses against our desires and inclinations, but it consistently moves the reader toward formation by Christ and identity in him. This book will strengthen and help any reader who approaches it in humility and good faith."

BARNABAS PIPER, Author, *Hoping for Happiness*; Assistant Pastor, Immanuel Nashville

"Justin Poythress biblically tackles what our culture seems to be continually obsessed with—identity. He has written a gospel antidote to the poisonous cultural fascination of searching inside yourself to discover your true identity. This book will be enormously helpful to any follower of Christ who wrestles with important questions about who they are and what in the world they're supposed to be doing."

SHELBY ABBOTT, Author; Speaker (Campus Ministries)

"Justin has given us a valuable contribution to the literature on finding your identity in Jesus. He explains, in simple terms, the philosophies and narratives of the past and present while subjecting them to a biblical analysis, and then goes on to offer a good framework for a pathway forward."

MATT FULLER, Author, *Be True to Yourself*; Senior Minister, Christ Church Mayfair, London